PRAISE FOR FLASH'S SONG

"FROM THE author of *Lauren's Story: An American Dog in Paris*, comes another beautiful tale of the power of love and the healing against all odds. [*Flash's*] *Song* speaks not only to the power of love and the human heart in healing, but also to the connection between humans and animals. This is a beautiful memoir, whose insights into dogs, love, and the intangible connection to all life will keep you turning the pages and lift your heart."

—DR. MARTY BECKER, "America's Veterinarian"

"THIS IS a very unusual and very beautiful book because it is filled with both heart and wisdom. Reading the story of Flash and Kay is like having a conversation with life. The rewar~~d~~ ~~f~~ ~~t~~he reader are similar to the lessons learned ~~f~~ iences. But Kay and Flash's story make it l~~e~~ time enriching our lives and making them

SIEGEL, MD, author of
The Art of Healing and *A Book of Miracles*

"IN MY opinion, Kay Pfaltz is brilliant: as an author, as a human being—one who fully understands what it means to love, the deepest, most expansive kind that includes all life. She is an artist of the highest moral and spiritual ranking. *Flash's Song* is magnificent, beautifully written from the Heart of Love within all, skillfully presented with a perfect combination of wisdom and humor. This is a book to keep close, return to often, and give to everyone you care about."

—RITA M. REYNOLDS, author of
Blessing the Bridge and *Ask the Cow*

"*FLASH'S SONG* reminds us that with love and faith, nothing is impossible."

—SUSAN WILSON, author of *One Good Dog,*
The Dog Who Danced, and *A Man of His Own*

"I HAVE admired Kay's writing for so many years—what a gift she has for helping us connect to animals and see and feel the beauty and wonder they bring into our lives. Like *Lauren's Story, Flash's Song* is a gem, not to be missed. If you have ever loved an animal, you will feel a kinship with Kay as she so beautifully describes that precious gift of unconditional love that they give us. If you have ever grieved the loss of an animal friend, Kay understands the depth of that loss."

—JUDY CARMAN, author of *Peace to*
All Beings: Veggie Soup for the Chicken's Soul

"I FOUND that reading *Flash's Song* before going to bed was very soothing. This is a beautiful book, profound in its simplicity and love. This is a book that brings great comfort and perhaps the real miracles are within its magical pages."

—JUDY NELSON, author of *Choices* and *Love Match*

"THERE ARE few writers in existence who touch my heart more than Kay Pfaltz. . . . This book grabs us from the first page to the last and takes us into a sacred space where there is harmony on earth and poetry in the universe and love, love, love. Read it now!"

—AMELIA KINKADE, author of *Straight from*
the Horse's Mouth and *The Language of Miracles*

"NONHUMAN ANIMALS (a.k.a. 'animals') can teach us numerous lessons about trust, forgiveness, dedication, peace, and love. For many people, dogs play this vital role in character building. And, the same goes for Kay Pfaltz. *Flash's Song,* a deeply inspirational and moving book that covers our complete emotional landscape, shows clearly how a 'salamander' wiener dog called Flash taught these and other lessons to Kay. His journey is a heartwarming reminder of just who other animals truly are when we open our hearts to them and allow them to pierce our souls."

—MARC BEKOFF, author of *The Emotional Lives of Animals* and *Why Dogs Hump and Bees Get Depressed*

"*FLASH'S SONG* reminds us of the uniqueness of all beings, and their capacity to touch our hearts."

—JONATHAN BALCOMBE, author of *The Exultant Ark*

"*FLASH'S SONG* takes us on Kay Pfaltz's uplifting journey with a loving and often fearless dachshund. In times that are often cynical or despairing, give yourself a respite. This book will uplift your spirits and broaden your acceptance of what is possible when you open your heart to the love freely given by a small pup in a big world."

—ALLEN ANDERSON, author of *A Dog Named Leaf*

"FLASH LOVED to sing, and in this book you will hear his song in happy times and sad. You will hear it still once you've closed the book."

—JERRY STEMNOCK, *Doxie Delight*

FLASH'S SONG

*How One Small Dog Turned into
One Big Miracle*

KAY PFALTZ

SKYHORSE PUBLISHING

Author's note: Some names and places have been changed.

Skyhorse Publishing books may be purchased in bulk at special discounts for sales promotion, corporate gifts, fund-raising, or educational purposes. Special editions can also be created to specifications. For details, contact the Special Sales Department, Skyhorse Publishing, 307 West 36th Street, 11th Floor, New York, NY 10018 or info@skyhorsepublishing.com.

Skyhorse® and Skyhorse Publishing® are registered trademarks of Skyhorse Publishing, Inc.®, a Delaware corporation.

Visit our website at www.skyhorsepublishing.com.

10 9 8 7 6 5 4 3 2 1

Library of Congress Cataloging-in-Publication Data is available on file.

Cover design by Marie Doucette
Cover photo by Ted Pfaltz

Print ISBN: 978-1-63450-256-6
Ebook ISBN: 978-1-5107-0204-2

Printed in the United States of America

To Ted,
Who loved Flash

And to the memory of
Rebecca Moravec

and to Chloe, Mosby, Yogi, Tasy, Dream,
and Tippy,
and all those who go on before us,
becoming bright lights in the dark,
leading the way for us to follow

Love is the affinity which links and draws together the elements of the world . . . Love, in fact, is the agent of universal synthesis.

—PIERRE TEIHARD DE CHARDIN

PROLOGUE

THERE WERE THE SOUNDS OF BEING ALIVE: THE BIRDS calling back and forth on a sundrenched day or the buzz of a fly. A chain saw coughing up the still air. After a summer shower there were cars in the distance moving along slick roads to unknown destinations, and their seemingly aimless traffic would get me thinking how none of us has any real knowledge of our destinies. We believe the dreams of childhood, but how many of these come to be? Still, we grow to love our little lives, the intimate clutter of a home, the backyard mud of winter calling to spring, even memories of a relationship that might have been. And that particular era into which we were born stretches before us turning back on itself again and again into timeless space. I've heard it said that time doesn't exist and there are moments when I know this is true . . . a déjà vu, or . . . sometimes when I stand very still on a clear spring day and he comes back to me.

At night there were the unexplained creaks of the house, or a bare branch scraping against the windowpane. Sometimes just the silence of the dark itself. But the best sound of all was the light sleeping breath of the dogs beside me. For so long a sound I took for granted, until our lives turned upside down.

Why does it take so long to realize the beauty of what we have, of what we have always had? Why does it so often take death, if even a figurative death of some part of ourselves, to cherish all, great and small alike?

For me, it took a tiny dog with a giant spirit to awaken me from unconscious slumber. Like many before me, I had walked with cardboard shadows, not realizing that at any time I chose I could cut them loose. I walked through the darkness of fear, unaware that beyond my grief awaited something vaster, yet somehow understanding that going through was my only way out. And while no one escapes the footfalls of fate, there is a depth one reaches only in sorrow. Out of this sorrow we are either crushed, unable to accept life's ruptures, or awakened into a state of grace.

CHAPTER 1

Love

Where there is the greatest love, there are always miracles.
—WILLA CATHER

THE THING ABOUT MIRACLES IS THAT THEY'RE ALL AROUND us. Just like love. True love and miracles go hand in hand. La Rochefoucauld said that true love is like seeing ghosts: we all talk about it, but few of us have ever seen one. Same thing with miracles. They say Jesus performed them and I guess the people saw, but that was a while ago and I wasn't around to take notes. Like love, miracles are hard to see, but easy to feel. They come when we're not expecting them; they come almost like a whisper or a shadow. We never know when because a miracle can befall us when we're doing laundry or cutting flowers, and because it comes in mundane moments, we miss it . . . until we wake up.

All miracles are born of love. Yet it seems we need the thorn's pierce before we can appreciate the scent of the rose. Yin and yang, dark and light, ebb and flow, each moment holds both the sorrow and the joy. And maybe we can only truly taste joy after we've drunk our share of sorrow. In my middle years I found my life, time and again, blessed by miracles. But this period of grace did not arrive without first summoning those disruptive forces—bearers of pain—which serve to awaken each of us. Sometimes they have to conk us over the head to get our attention, because while most people will tell you they want spiritual enlightenment, when fear and pain come knocking, those same people are on the first boat to Jamaica to drink rum drinks with little umbrellas in them and dig holes in the sand to stick their heads in. Or so it was with me. Which only means I was prime to get conked.

As with much of my life, it began with a dog. A long shiny piece of black licorice named Flash.

Flash was a gift, a gift born of love. Well, love and a pinch of dysfunction. It was my sister, Amy, who gave me my first dog, Lauren. Lauren had been a skin-and-bones starving beagle who turned up in severe need of medical treatment under Amy's front porch. Although plagued by illness her entire life, Lauren became the great love of my life, living in Paris with me and dining out in many a French restaurant. Because of this great gift, I felt I would remain forever indebted to Amy and at some point I decided that remaining in debt to one's older sister could have its disadvantages. And yet it would again be Amy who gave me Flash, this time paying a friend to fly out to Arizona, where she then lived, to carry Flash back to me in Virginia.

Amy lay awake night after sleepless night afraid of the grief I'd endure when Lauren died, quite convinced I would try any number of methods (turn on the oven and open the door, swallow a bottle of pills, jump out the window, fill in the blank, she had a whole list) to follow Lauren to wherever she went. Our arguments took on a similar flavor.

"I don't want another dog," I'd say each time.

"Think of the silver lining," she'd insist.

"The what?"

"The silver lining."

I'd look around my house and see stinkbugs bombing about, but no silver lining. "I don't see it."

"The silver lining is that the dark part of the cloud—the grief and need that causes you to reach out and welcome another dog—"

"But that's just it, I'm not reaching out."

". . . is also what in time will be a balm to your soul in years to come," she'd continue, completely dismissing any opinion I might offer. "That little shimmering edge around the darkness will grow. There's always a silver lining behind the pain. And then there's also the fact that you've rescued another animal in need."

On a beautiful morning in May I had held Lauren in my arms as she died. But that's a different story.

The silver lining was the beauty behind the pain, and this new dog, according to Amy, was to symbolize for me the silver lining behind much of life. Amy's silver lining lecture got so predictable it would follow just about anything I could think to say, regardless of content.

"I don't ever want another dog."

"But think of the silver *lining*."

"I think I'll develop a pathological obsession with chocolate-covered hazelnuts," and without missing a beat, she'd say, "Think of the silver *lining*." She kept up in this fashion, until one day, finding me acquiescing in a moment of weakness, she grabbed the first dog she found, literally dumped from a car, and sent me the small black emissary of healing. My silver lining.

I always felt this one example exemplified my sister's love for me, to say nothing of her faith in my coping skills.

It was October 27. I remember it well. Amy said her friend Scotty would meet me in the parking lot in front of Barnes & Noble and there she would hand over Flash. I drove up in my old pickup truck and saw Scotty holding a smooth-haired miniature black dachshund on her lap. From a distance I remember thinking he resembled a large salamander. He looked a little slippery, and he looked a little crooked. Scotty and I said hello and she nodded her head down to the placid salamander. "This is Flash. Amy said he's to become your silver lining, whatever that's supposed to mean." But before I could respond, more words rushed from her mouth. "I'm really worried. He won't look up at me anymore. I think something's wrong. Or worse, he's mad at me and I can't go through life with someone holding a vendetta against me. Even if it is a dachshund."

"He doesn't really look the type," I said, trying to reassure her, but she didn't seem convinced.

"I don't know. First he bonded with Amy, followed her around the house and everywhere. Then I take him away from her after he's already been dumped by his original family for who knows what stupid reason. Too expensive to feed probably."

"He's pretty small," I said, taking in his smooth body, which couldn't have been much more than twelve or fourteen inches long. "Can't really see him eating through bags of dog food."

"No, no it happens. Dog chews up a chair leg. Let's dump him. Vet bills too expensive. Give him away! Bites the neighbor. *Euthanize him!*" She was on a roll. "It happens all the time," she said. I nodded then. She was right; it happened. "Now he's bonded with me. All that love and togetherness on the plane and, poor little runt, I have to give him up." It sounded like a mail-order husband from Russia or something that hadn't worked out.

"Maybe he's just sad or confused," I said.

"Oh, God. No wonder he won't look up at me. He must think he made some humongous mistakes along the way."

"*Flash,*" I said softly, addressing him this time.

"Flash boy, you haven't done anything wrong. *Please* don't be mad at me. I was only trying to help."

"I think he knows that," I said, trying to put Scotty's mind at ease. "They understand our intentions."

"Please don't be mad," she said again to Flash.

"He's sensitive, isn't he?" I asked, eyeing the small dog on her lap, who kept taking surreptitious peeps at me without, it seemed, wanting me to notice.

"Yes. He was so good on the plane. Well, he was drugged. He may be a little groggy for a while. Maybe *that's* it!" She seemed at once greatly relieved by Flash's drug-induced state.

"You won't be passed around anymore," I said to Flash. Then to Scotty, "Thank you so much."

"Nothing to thank me for. Amy sent me a ticket. I got a mini vacation and a chance to see your sister. You know, I don't think too many sisters would do that for each other," she said. Then with some reluctance I thought, she passed Flash over to me.

I held him in my arms for the first time and he looked up.

"Take good care of him."

"I will," I answered.

"I have faith. I have faith that you will."

Faith. What did it mean? Could I share her same faith? Here I was taking over the care of an animal I knew nothing about, committing to take care of him for the rest of his life.

"Please don't be mad!" Scotty called after us as I started to walk away. "She'll take good care of you."

"Thanks so much," I said again and, carrying Flash, I walked back to my truck. Once in the cab, I set Flash on the seat beside me and really looked at him. That first real look at his face is laced into my soul. With his squinty, sedated eyes he stared up at me with partially pricked ears and tipped his head to one side. It was a curious look, a questioning look, and a slightly worried look. But there was also the beginning of trust, perhaps the trust all animals must give to the humans who assume the role of guardian throughout their lives.

"It's okay, Flash," I said softly. "This will be your last home."

He looked at me and I sensed he seemed to be waiting for more. Maybe Scotty's neurosis had gotten to me. "I promise you I'll take good care of you forever. No matter what," I said, and I could feel Scotty somewhere heaving a sigh of relief. I wasn't so sure about Flash.

We drove off together in this fashion, me talking quietly to him, reaching my hand over to stroke his shiny back, and him cocking his head with its dazed expression to regard this latest person to take up command in his dachshund life.

Before taking Flash to his new home, however, I pulled up to the wine, bread, and cheese shop that I had created ten years earlier after returning to Virginia from Paris and finding no decent wine, bread, cheese, or chocolate. I stocked it with those items and named it Basic Necessities, hoping people wouldn't stop in seeking toothpaste or toilet paper. Eventually it morphed into a café and as it grew I took in partners to share the responsibility and expenses so that now I only worked part-time to supplement my writing. My current partners, Bev and Keith, lived on an organic farm one mile from the little shop. It was a marriage made in heaven, and I felt blessed to have them. We could offer organic produce more than half the year, and I felt the pride of telling diners not only that their veggies were local and organic, but that they were picked a mere hour or so ago from a farm down the road. We hired a wonderful chef, Sallie Justice, who understood our philosophy, and again I felt grateful for she brought elegance and professionalism into our small kitchen.

I carried Flash in my arms. But before I reached the door to show him off, Marie, who'd been working off and on for ten years, came rushing out to greet us.

"Oh my God! Look at the *wiener dog!*"

I turned and looked behind me, not comprehending right away.

"You and the wiener dog look just alike!"

Flash had a beautiful black face with two brown spots above his eyes which I called his umlaut, after the Germanic dots that sometimes appear above a vowel. The umlaut gave definition to his dark face, helping me easily read his expressions and understand his wants and needs. Perhaps it was our similar dark coloring that inspired Marie's remark, but I have to assume that, apart from this, the wiener dog and I did not look just alike, for Flash had the biggest overbite of any dog I had ever seen, his upper jaw and nose extending out well over an inch beyond his short lower jaw. In this respect, neither did he resemble other dachshunds. His profile was funny with its comic flaws, more like a bucked-tooth caricature of a dachshund than a real dachshund. At least until it became a face known to me. Then it was a face—perhaps for its very flaws—that I could only ever love.

"Meet Flash," I said as I walked into the shop. "The latest addition to my family."

The staff all came out to see him, and as Mae, Marian, Marie, Sarah, and Hayley all reached hands down simultaneously to touch Flash, I saw that he didn't shrink away from the strange hands but observed each person. Perhaps he was sizing everyone up. The afternoon light came in through the shop's front window, and I saw a funny shadow against the wall: Flash and me, merged into one entity.

Just then, Rosie, one of our best customers, walked over and I gave introductions again, and soon we were all talking at once, exclaiming over Flash.

"The love the animals give us is like none other," Rosie said, stroking Flash's back. I looked at her and thought, yes, how true. "Do you ever wonder what lies ahead for you and him? Taking him in, how he'll change your life. . . ."

"What journeys you'll travel together, because of each other," Mae said.

I nodded, feeling an odd current travel up my spine. "I don't know him now, but I know I'll come to love him."

"I guess we find love where we can," Rosie said. "And love finds us when it's right."

Chapter 2

Welcome, Flash

No trumpets sound when the important decisions of our life are made. Destiny is made silently.
                                        —Agnes de Mille

Once home, Flash seemed to fit in almost instantly. My brother, Ted, joked that he would since anything was preferable to the crack house he'd come from. Ted surmised that Flash was the result of a drug deal gone bad. Maybe, but all we really knew was that a car had pulled over to the side of the road, and a small dog dumped out.

How lives turn on tiny events that at the time are no more than the fabric of that hour or moment. What might have become of this tiny dog had Amy not been in the car behind? Would he have become easy fodder for predators? Would he have starved to death or died of dehydration in the harsh Arizona desert? For a while these thoughts became a preoccupation of mine, my heart constricting as I thought of the multitude of different possibilities, of a tiny, smooth-coated dachshund navigating the landscape—cacti quills and coyotes—all on his own.

"I mean what if it hadn't been you?" I sort of half-whimpered to Amy.

"Kay," my sister said patiently. "What if Caesar hadn't crossed the Rubicon, or what if George Washington hadn't crossed the Delaware?"

"What?"

"They *did*. That's the point."

"We'd be drinking tea and speaking with English accents?" I offered, a little late.

Amy sighed like I was the biggest moron ever to rewrite history.

"Maybe it's the accident of fate." I'd read it somewhere.

"Fate is no accident," Amy answered. "Any more than courage is or generosity or kindness. The point is that you wouldn't be worrying about him because you wouldn't know him. And whether fate is already written or not doesn't matter. We work with what is . . . and accept what is."

I pondered this and realized that at some point after receiving the gift of Flash, it would perhaps serve me to let go of trying to understand; to accept the fact that no human will ever completely understand another, not a husband his wife, not a lover his beloved, not even a sibling his genetic analogue. Perhaps that's why we invent multiple gods who are capable of understanding, and perhaps the true partner is this god or goddess, the being with whom we will forever seek union, for isn't all love the search for oneness with something greater than ourselves?

When I said this to Amy, she answered back in one of her less sarcastic responses that yes, this was true but yet, paradoxically, the love we seek resides within us all, not outside of us. If we can but tap into it, if only for seconds at a time, we shift the paradigm. But I'm getting ahead of my story.

The neighborhood where Flash was dumped was one of those less-than-savory ones in Tucson known for harboring crack houses ("and odd, somewhat rubbery, conformationally incorrect, backyard-breeder, tiny dachshunds," Ted had said)—probably not the sort of neighborhood in which you'd want to raise your toddler.

Here in the gentle mountains of central Virginia, patrolling the yard for voles and moles, Flash must have felt he'd won the doggie lotto. He had a dog-door and could come and go from the house freely into his fenced backyard. There were flowering shrubs, fruit trees, and an old apple crate, one of the large ones that, upside-down, served as a table of sorts. There were flowers and birds who I fed all year round. When my old bird feeder fell apart I'd begun construction on a new one, but all that stood was a large cross with one feeder hanging from it, and bells that I bought for each of the dogs. I hoped the neighbors didn't think I was trying to convert the birds to Christianity.

In later years there would be my Writing Room at the end of the yard, bordered by flower gardens. And there was a little pine tree I'd planted in the spot where Lauren had taken her last steps. I'd named the tree Lauren and will avoid mentioning Amy's comments on this particular topic. Flash loved that little tree. He would hunt for hours, rooting around the yard, then flop down, panting hard beneath Lauren. Other times he would roll on his back in the grass in joy. Sometimes he'd race in to where I sat working to tell me about his day.

The first time this happened, I was writing at my desk. Muted gold light, liquid light filled the room, and I was warm from its touch. My mind was filled not so much with finished outcomes as with anticipations and infinite possibilities. Into this still scene ran Flash, leaping up onto the loveseat right beside me and shoving his long, dark, and crooked snout against my arm, distorting the words I was writing with pen

11

and ink. In the early days, before I had the separate building for my Writing Room, my office doubled as my writing studio and it was pretty cramped, the loveseat where he stood nearly touching my desk.

He pushed my arm again.

"Almost finished. Just wait a sec."

He pushed a third time.

"*Quit it*," I said, concentrating on one last line without looking at him.

Then I stopped. There I was wishing to write about life when life was sitting right beside me, asking to be seen. I took my hands from the paper and turned to Flash. He cocked his head to the side. He was panting lightly, his mouth open showing the discrepancy between his upper and lower jaws. He smiled at me with his tongue lolling partially out of his mouth and his tail brushing back and forth on the loveseat. It was long and thin like a black whip, with a crooked end. In that way Flash was symmetrical. Crooked snout, crooked tail. The slanted afternoon light came in through the window behind and gave him a silvered glow. His dark eyes bored into my own.

"Alright. Tell me all about it," I said and he hunched up his back and dug his front feet into the loveseat cushion. I watched his body, a shiny black shoe, wiggle wildly, side to side. "Picture a muskrat humping along through the reeds," was how Ted once described Flash, and he wasn't far off the mark. I stared back into Flash's dark-complected face.

"So what do you think about life?

He made a little *grrr*ing sound and kept digging up the loveseat.

"Flash, you have a forever home now."

"Waarip, rep, rep. Awwwoooooooo," he replied in his soprano voice, and I felt the emotion go from my heart to his and back again.

Sometimes we played "chase" in the house, with me always chasing him, never the other way around. I slunk slowly, stealthily across the room on all fours as he peeked out from behind an armchair. As long as I was moving, he was okay, *grrr*ing at me with pricked ears and alert body, ready to flee the predator if the predator got too close. If I stopped, however, and remained still, he became nervous and soon began to bark. It was then that I'd leap forward, chasing after him, and this was the part he loved. Around and around he raced, circling the woodstove in our small house, skidding across rugs and floors as he did. When tired, we collapsed together in one pile, and I'd stroke his heaving sides as his tail flumped the ground a few satisfied times.

Whenever I stretched or did yoga on the floor, he'd stand over me, shoving his snout into my face or hand to be rubbed. I didn't need much of an excuse to stop my exercises. He looked funny from my supine position, but I knew what he was saying to me. He loved having me down on his level.

Before dinnertime, Flash would become especially excited and race to the corner by the woodstove where I kept a basket full of toys. There he'd snatch one out and dash to the middle of the room where he'd shake the toy (I think he liked to believe he was helping the dinner preparation by snapping the neck of a chicken) while his ears smacked against the side of his head, and that funny flapping noise was a sound I came to love.

When Flash ate, his heels turned in nearly touching each other, and his bad conformation was particularly noticeable. "Cow hocks" is the phrase used to describe this condition in horses. I don't know if there's a similar term for malformed dachshunds. At night I called to him to go out even though he had the doggie-door. He would always turn and sniff the spot where he had raised his leg. He was proud of his pee, prouder still of his penis. I liked to listen for the soft flap of the dog-door and the patter of feet as I sat at my desk or stood brushing my teeth before bed, the sound getting closer and closer as he came to find me. Then I'd tuck him into the bed and he would sleep curled on his side. I'd stroke him and sing him his own special song: "He's so fine, he's so fine, and I'm so glad that he's all mine." I'd put my mouth to his eyes and kiss him. If I woke in the night, I'd watch him sleep. His nose was so long, I often saw the very end of it pushed up against my pillow and twisted to the side.

It was while I was in Paris that Ted taught Flash how to sing. I never knew exactly how he did this, although for his part, I think a bottle of wine was involved. All I know is what he told me. He began by stating the word "sing" whenever Flash became particularly shrill and insistent on something outside. He used repetition and consistency until Flash, not stupid, put two and two together, eager in his desire to perform a job and please.

Perhaps in search of praise, perhaps because he enjoyed it, Flash began to sing at any opportunity. Yet at first Ted and I had to get him started by *Oooohhhhhh*ing and *Whoooooooooo*-ing, although always ever careful not to be overly conspicuous (an oxymoron, no doubt) lest we be taken away by the men in white coats and put in rubber rooms. Within seconds, Flash would begin a chorus of his own—a sort of let-me-show-you-how-it's-done rendition.

After a while all we had to do was say, "*Sing, Flash,*" and he would fling his head back, his uneven mouth now an instrument for a melodic tune of his own devising. Ted and I reinforced Flash's natural propensity to sing with applause after each song, and I think he could feel our hearts smiling as he sang.

I'd be at my desk working when Flash would fly in to tell me of his adventures. I'd say in a serious tone, "Flash, I don't suppose you want to sing . . ." And with that cue, he would fill the small room with a melodious "*Whoooooohhhhhh.*" As time went by I needed only to say, "I don't suppose . . ." and he knew the rest, belting out choruses like he was auditioning for *American Idol.* Afterward I always said to him the same words: "Thank you, Flash. Thank you for that beautiful song."

And so our life had begun . . . one day turning into a week, a week turning into a month . . . then a year, invincible time against which I would later try so hard to fight.

CHAPTER 3

The Work Day

The most satisfying thing in life is to have been able to give a large part of one's self to others.
—PIERRE TEILHARD DE CHARDIN

DOGS THRIVE WHEN GIVEN JOBS. A GERMAN SHEPHERD might have the job of guarding the house, for instance. Or a Chihuahua . . . our world is fraught with discrimination. A dachshund is a fine house guard, but an even finer mouse patroller. Therefore, Flash quickly took up this line of work without my suggesting it. Dachshunds were bred to hunt badgers, but in the absence of badgers in our home, Flash fixated on every ambulatory rodent who took up residence within our walls. Yet because I respect all beings, I did not so much want him to catch the mice as give them such a good chase. I thought they'd look for a nicer landlady. I had no idea how many mice there were until Flash came along. He'd sit and stare at one particular hole in the knotty wood paneling, tilting his head when he heard some sound I didn't hear. When he heard the noise or picked up a rodent vibration, he began to dig, dig, dig on the floor. These determined digs seemed futile to me—or perhaps poignantly valiant—for our floor was made of terra-cotta tile. But I never said a word.

Out in the yard, as well as rooting around for voles and moles, he loved to chase birds and butterflies and, because I saw he had little chance of catching them, I did not discourage him. I learned to tell his "butterfly bark" from his "bird bark," which was more high-pitched and shrill.

The first time I saw him do this, he was waiting under a Rose of Sharon bush, believing that in his shrubbery camouflage he was invisible. When an unsuspecting finch floated by, he charged the quarry, leaping in the air and yipping as he did, which only served to send the alarm out to all the other birds to fly away. I never corrected his hunting tactics; if he hadn't inadvertently warned the birds, I would have.

The first spring after I adopted Flash, I planted a small cherry tree for him, happy with the thought of blossoms in March and sweet fruit in June. It was a Napoleon cherry, which I found appropriate for one of small size but such colossal spirit.

Flash fit into my life, and what's more, Flash was portable. I held him in the crook of my left arm and stroked his tummy with my right hand, while his narrow, dainty hind feet crossed, one over the other, and his flat front paws, so good at digging, hung limp. He'd never admit to it but he loved being held like that. He did, however, admit to a real dislike of being left home alone. He followed me around the house when I was getting ready to go out and as I slipped out the front door, looking back at him, I easily understood the look in his eyes: a mixture of entreaty and fear. Perhaps he thought he was being abandoned again.

Margaret Mead said, "One of the oldest human needs is having someone wonder where you are when you don't come home at night." It was great for my ego to have the major welcoming committee when I returned home—Flash flying around the house and wiggling like some kind of large, high-energy, designer lizard—but I couldn't forget his worried face, and it was that look in his eyes that was largely responsible for my decision to take him with me whenever possible.

Weighing in at ten to twelve pounds depending on how many rodents he'd found that day, Flash could be carried anywhere, and this included my sneaking him into restaurants where dogs were forbidden or onto airplanes and trains. Flash sat beside me in restaurants, just as Lauren once had in Paris, albeit hidden away in the mesh travel bag I had once used for her.

The first time we snuck into a restaurant in the US I left him in the bag and slipped him scraps of food from my plate. But the second time, even though the bag was vented, I sensed he was getting stuffy. Halfway through the meal, I unzipped the bag and out popped his small, black, pointed head. His lip was puffed up, his ears flattened back. He resembled a pterodactyl.

It was fall, and every restaurant that year seemed to offer some version of butternut squash ravioli. Some ravioli were instantly recognizable as the "food service" kind, coming to restaurants frozen, laden with preservatives, while others oozed that description-defying deliciousness, made-from-scratch look and taste as if the Italian mother whose recipe had been handed down through generations was back in the kitchen nodding her approval at each returning licked-clean plate. I quartered my ravioli and fed Flash bites discreetly, stroking his head and hoping not to draw attention to our table. A glass of Aglianico from Campania and a green salad with simple walnuts and garlic afterward complemented the pasta. When I'd finished, our waitress came back and asked if I wanted coffee or dessert. She didn't ask if Flash might like some water, nor did she tell us we had to leave because one of us was not allowed in the restaurant, so I assumed she had simply not seen him. What I observed was that about eight times out of ten, the waiters or waitresses never noticed him sitting there beside me. Maybe one doesn't see what one doesn't expect. If they did see him, they only asked if they could pet him, for they were not the ones concerned about the health inspector; they were only concerned with delivering food, making tips, and trying to earn a living.

There is something infinitely fine about dining with those you love—it's a nourishment that settles not only into your stomach but also into your psyche, eventually lodging somewhere in memory and while perhaps the path of memory, ever changing with the years, is formed in the mind, it's accessed with a special key, custom-made by the heart.

The restaurant scene may have spoiled Flash because I came home one day to find no greeter at the door. People who tell you that animals can't reason probably have never lived with an animal. Jeffrey Moussaieff Masson and many other writers and scholars have, with countless real-life examples, shattered the Cartesian view of animals as unfeeling machines incapable of emotions.

"Flash?" I called, assuming he was out in the yard and just hadn't heard me drive up. Then I saw the trash spilled out in the kitchen. I walked back to my office and there I found him curled in a very small ball on the loveseat, as though he were trying to dissolve. His head was lowered as he looked up at me and I could see the whites of his eyes.

"Flash. What's this all about?"

I saw the end of his tail twitch a few times between his legs, but it moved out of nervousness rather than joy. I left the room to clean up the mess. I kept separate bags for recycling and he had upended the one for paper, his object of desire probably the empty almond milk carton. Out of the corner of my eye, I saw him slink away and out the doggie-door, his tail hanging low, skimming the floor.

Twenty minutes later I walked to the end of the yard where I found him excavating. When he saw me approach he held his tail low and it waved back and forth a few feeble times. "How's it going?" I asked as I surveyed his hole. He looked up at me and back down into his hole. I knelt next to him, reaching out my hand to his long back.

"It's okay," I said softly. "Sometimes in life we need to investigate a little to understand." I looked at him but he wasn't looking back at me. "Even if this investigation involves the . . . trash. It's okay, Flash. It's all okay."

He sank into the soft grass then, flopping on his side and I heard him emit a little sigh. "It's okay, my friend," I continued. "I tell you what, how about if I take you to work when I go?" He understood my tone. His tail beat the earth then he hopped up and began once more to dig.

That night I lay in bed listening to the silence of the night. Into this silence there came another sound—the scratching, rattling noises of a mouse rustling about in the kitchen. A sound I knew well. I turned to Flash beside me, about to say, "Mice," in the special tone I used for mice, but he was out. Off duty.

CHAPTER 4

Dachshund Life

And do not change. Do not divert your love from visible things. But go on loving what is good, simple and ordinary; animals and things and followers, and keep the balance true.

—RAINER MARIA RILKE

BECAUSE I LIVED ALONE, FLASH RECEIVED THE FULL, UNDILUTED force of my attention. He also received love and spoiling from my family as well as friends and neighbors.

I walked him daily and, in the warm months, we passed neighbors out tending vegetable gardens or, in the case of Nora down the road, riding bikes.

"Hey, Kay, hey. How's it going?" Nora asked as she pedaled up beside us one day.

"Going good." I smiled. "How about you?"

"Good, good. I can't complain." Nora's face was smooth and dark with a smile so white it was as if she was lit from within. She pulled her hair straight so it lay with just enough curl at the edge and made her look like the Hollywood stars of the forties.

"How are the kids?" I asked, because Nora taught at the local elementary school.

"The kids," she began. "Bad as they write, you know sometimes they surprise you."

"Yeah?" I asked, trying to sound hopeful.

"I had a boy last week writing stories about pancake kingdoms with syrup rivers where the knives and forks began to fight."

A vision of *Alice in Wonderland* merged with "Kubla Khan," I was about to exclaim, when a dark Buick roared by. I jerked Flash to my side fast but my heart was pounding. The car had come inches from hitting him.

"Lord, give me strength," Nora said under her breath.

Flash seemed oblivious to his close call, but I let out my breath and felt my heart beating hard.

"Why does he have to be like that?" Nora asked.

The driver of the Buick who had just blown a fine dust all over us was Mr. Jake, a retired man who lived up the hill beyond us. Behind my house lay thousands of acres of fields and forests, put into a conservation easement by a Mr. Craddock, and over which I could walk, but the driveway leading to Mr. Jake's house was one of the main gateways to this paradise. Right after I bought my house, I was eager to begin exploring the woods and the mystery that lay beyond.

I remember the first time I encountered Mr. Jake. I was walking with Lauren when the dark car came roaring down the drive. Its brakes screeched when the driver saw us and I watched as it slowly began backing up. I remember feeling a strange detachment as the ominous presence came toward us. I pulled Lauren to my side just like I did with Flash, and stood still, waiting, ready to offer a greeting, those insignificant but essential first forms of pleasantry by which we humans live. But my intuition, knowing more than my rational mind, was waving a red flag. In fact, it was jumping up and down shouting to me, "Tuck your tail and run!" I couldn't see in through the dark, tinted windows. But I listened as the window purred open and an odd voice came from inside.

"No trespassing," the voice said. "Get your dog off." The window rolled back shut, locking us out, and the car took off, churning up gravel in its wake.

It had been a blemish on our beautiful world, but the joy of being up in those hills outweighed the risk of encountering the car . . . and the voice. I wondered what had made him like that, if he'd always been so bitter and mean.

"The story is, he was kicked out of his company and has never forgiven the ones who did him wrong," Nora said, breaking my thoughts and answering the unspoken question.

"It's sad to see someone hardened like that. And no wife, no family?"

"Just himself, all anger and blame, like some prize float in the hostility parade."

"He sure made it hard for me when I first moved here."

"You were expecting apple pies?"

I smiled. "I was afraid to walk up there." I pulled on Flash's leash to keep him near me, as though Mr. Jake might come roaring by again.

"But not that afraid," Nora laughed, knowing I walked all over the back land.

"We've gotten used to it, but how does a person go through life like that? I wonder if there's anything we could do to help him. . . ."

"Have faith that he can change. That's about all."

23

"If change is what he wants," I added hesitantly. No sense pushing the river if the river was barreling down its own course in a dark Buick.

"That he can change, and faith that the good Lord will see to it," she continued without missing a beat. "Trust in the good Lord."

"Yeah," I said thinking that the good Lord seemed to slip up every now and again.

"He who hunts for flowers will find flowers, and he who loves weeds will find weeds," Nora said. I almost added, *And he who hunts for rodents . . .* as I glanced down at Flash. But I didn't, and Nora continued, "Pure thoughts, a pure life."

For some reason this struck a chord with me.

"And how's he doing?" she asked, pointing down at Flash.

"Flash?" I beamed. "I think his thoughts are very pure."

She smiled at me. "It all works out in the end. It always does."

Maybe so. I walked on with Flash beside me.

⁓

After Flash's exploration of the trash, I began taking him with me to work at Basic Necessities. There he developed quite a small following. Kids learned the days he'd be there and would race in shouting, "*Sing,* Flash! *Sing!*" in high-pitched voices Flash disliked. He'd charge the front door, barking and yipping at certain customers, which wasn't the best for business. But since dogs are often better judges of character than humans are, I was able to weed out some unsavory specimens with Flash's help.

Sims, the son of a German friend of mine, was particularly fond of Flash. He'd walk into the shop, and when he saw Flash he'd always say, "Hey, Flash. How's it going?" Then Sims would hold Flash on his lap and talk to him as if my little dachshund were no different from anyone else entering the shop. And perhaps he wasn't. I believe that animals and humans are more alike than different and if anything, that animals possess a greater, not lesser, emotional intelligence than humans, something that is hard for us to comprehend if we've never experienced emotions on that plane, and something that begins to take on great implications when applied to the current model of industrial farming.

I knew that, contrary to what many people said, Flash, like many dogs, understood time. He knew the days I worked at the shop, and he knew that they were different from the days I had to drive into town for errands. I could read the expressions that crossed his face and his body language as easily as he read my energy. He'd lie on his haunches, alert, watching me as I dressed and then rushed around, usually searching for my glasses. If I was gone for brief periods of time, he'd greet me at the door enthusiastically. But if I'd been gone for an extended trip—like once when I went to Paris without him—he was beside himself, peeing on me in excitement or pure emotion as I lifted him up against my chest.

It didn't take me long at all to realize that Flash's world was unique. Maybe animals live in different worlds than we humans do because they live without the constant chatter of the mind. They live for the present moment, understanding on some level that the simple moment is the best there is. Animals are in most cases more accepting and forgiving than the human animal appears to be. There is that old joke where a man asks God to bring him a mate who is enthusiastic, joyful, kind, loyal, grateful, accepting, forgiving, and will love him unconditionally throughout life. And God says, "Okay, I'll send you a dog."

A friend once said to me, "I want to live in Flash's world." "Flash's world" consisted of chasing butterflies from bush to bush, and elusive birds that he would never catch. It consisted of sleeping in bed under the covers because that is where he insisted on being; I called him my "undercover dog." The first time I saw him go undercover I was stunned. Lauren had never done that. I'd just thrown a soft blanket onto his dog bed. I watched as he shoved his long snout under the blanket, and with one deft toss it was covering his head. A few more tosses and he had it over his back with just his nose poking out. Who knows where he learned a trick like that, coming from the Arizona desert. Some of his efforts were better than others. And I'd find him with the blanket over his head, but his smooth-coated body exposed to the cold. I would pull the blanket so it covered him, and pat and rub his back as I did.

Flash's world also consisted of high-quality treats and frequent tummy rubs, and of singing songs that reverberated around our small house. He grew to love his life and bodily comforts to the extent that any small upset would write itself across his dachshund face. From the time he arrived in Virginia, it seemed nothing bad had ever happened in Flash's world.

One afternoon I stood outside in the yard watching him dig in the dirt like a child in the sandbox. Just as a mother stands above a crawling baby, knowing that that singular time cannot last forever, and knowing that that extension of self and heart that crawls across the floor will face grief, disappointment, even despair, so too did I stand poised in a place, knowing that to give into love now and know the joy it brings was also to accept the sorrow of later.

CHAPTER 5

Brave Heart

Courage is the art of being the only one who knows you're scared to death.

—HAROLD WILSON

EVEN THOUGH HE WAS SMALL, FLASH NEVERTHELESS HAD dominion over our household. He was brave to the point of rashness, exhibiting his fearlessness in exaggerated efforts to save me from potential predators—like badgers, or, in their absence, large Labrador retrievers, a breed that, contrary to what its eponymous name suggests, actually comes from Newfoundland.

One summer afternoon at a friend's house, I swam to the center of her pool alone except for huge and lovable Hank, a Labrador whose keenness for swimming was second only to his devotion to eating. Assuming that food-loving Hank presented a danger to me, Flash ran up and down the edges of the pool yipping anxiously.

"Flash, I'm okay!" I called from the water, laughing and enjoying the show. "Quite safe!" But my words as well as my proximity to the huge Lab did not reassure Flash, and in the next instant he jumped.

It was neither a practiced nor a pretty dive as his dachshund body, not exactly designed for swimming and definitely not for high diving, plunged into the water, belly touching down like a wayward plane. Flash submerged under the surface for seconds then resurfaced, kicking, paddling, and stroking valiantly toward me to rescue me from the killer whale masquerading as a Labrador.

I cut quickly through the water to reach him about the same time he realized he was in over his head and turned and headed back to the side of the pool. But without my aid he was unable to scramble out, and as I scooped him up and out, I watched him hang his head even before shaking the water from his sleek, wet coat. Had I then the awareness I do now, the incident might have seemed significant, a first clue to the life that would unfold for us in the years ahead. But I hadn't understood that Flash was truly trying to rescue me. I thought I was rescuing him. In the end, though, I suppose love means rescuing each other.

But it was my friend who really rescued him on that day. "Ask him if he wants to sing," she said, walking up to us and nudging me as Hank stepped out of the pool, shook his coat all over us, and then licked my hand but didn't try to eat me. Most of my friends knew singing was among Flash's favorite pastimes, and some of those friends, perhaps the ones of dubious hearing, declared he sang more harmoniously than Maria Callas and Renata Tebaldi combined.

"Flash?" I said in that special voice apposite to asking him to sing. "I don't suppose you want to sing. Flash, do you want to *sing*?" And with that he began a serenade, and as he was quickly joined by each of the other dogs in various stages of barking, whining, and yelping, his prior disgrace fell away like the water droplets from his long dachshund body.

Other than singing, Flash's favorite activity was chasing "the flash." The flash was the light reflected most often from my watch, but it could also be a laser beam. I would trace the light across the surface of a rug and Flash would dash after it, for as long as I'd let him. It had first happened accidentally one afternoon when I was sitting outside reading in the sun, and the light catching the crystal of my watch created the flash of light that captivated him. It was a tiny fairy dancing from one blade of grass to the next, magical in its power to persist despite Flash's best attempts at capture. He would dig up the earth where the little square of light had fallen, then back up to see whether he'd "got it." If the light still sparkled, he'd dig and dig and take big bites of earth, his nose brown from dirt and grass tips hanging from the sides of his mouth. He never tired of chasing the light. But I did. At least in the early days. And in these moments, I'd have to say, "You *got* it, Flash," and praise him until he stood back surveying the flashless grass, satisfied with his work.

His acts of bravery were not limited to saving me from drowning or from hungry Labrador retrievers, however. He would regularly charge dogs five and six times his size, barking his high-pitched yip as he did. These attacks would always find me running in an adrenaline-spiked sprint close behind yelling, "Flash! *No!*" Into my dreams would slip these moments, the kind of dreams where you try to run forward but can't go fast enough or can't move your legs at all. And always I awoke calling out his name over and over.

Yes, he was brave. But beneath the bravado lay a sensitivity not celebrated in our culture, yet more endearing to me than any Napoleonic acts of bravery. If the path to strength is vulnerability, Flash and I still had lessons to learn. I think sometimes we're afraid to let ourselves love too much, afraid someone will come and take it away.

CHAPTER 6

Chance Encounters

The important thing is not to think much, but to love much; and so, do that which best stirs you to love.
—Sainte Thérèse d'Ávila

When I look back on my life with Flash, I see lazy days filled with sunshine; days that stretched out long like the summer light, like the days I knew in childhood that I thought would last forever. Now time feels rushed. I wonder if that carefree pace of the past was all an illusion or did we really spend long hours together doing nothing but sitting and being? Maybe it is both the past's power and prank, to be able to erase any sense of worry or distress. Perhaps nostalgia's very command lies in its ability to trick us into faulty remembering. And if this is so, I guess I don't really mind.

I know those early days were not all roses. There was still the sorrow over Lauren, grief of a sort that is not extinguished overnight. Flash too had sleeping demons yet to heal, real fears of which I was at first unaware.

The reasons why anyone gets a dog—for companionship, to rescue another in need, to give and receive unconditional love, to learn presence, or simply to know joy—are purely conceptual next to the inevitable heartbreak with which our hearts are forced into intimacy along the way.

One day my friend Patty phoned and I didn't realize then that her call would change the course of our lives. "There's a tiny, mangy beagle at the SPCA," Patty said. "She's been there a while, and no one's even asked after her. Probably because of her condition. She's scheduled to be euthanized."

I felt compassion for a little dog who had most likely done nothing to deserve this fate. Yet I didn't want another beagle. It was too soon after Lauren; one doesn't replace one life with another. I also wanted Flash to be an only dog for a while, lavished with attention, but when Patty called again that same week and said that the little beagle's time was up, I felt something shift inside. There was sadness and my heart was speaking louder than my mind, speaking to me of a small dog about to die. I looked to Flash.

"Should we at least go see?" He looked back at me with pricked ears and cocked his head to the side. "Would you like a sister to play with?" And with that he began digging up the ground—in this case, my good Persian carpet.

When Patty and I arrived at the SPCA, I was taken to the isolation unit where the tiny, mangy beagle was being held while Patty walked up and down looking in the outside runs. What I saw when I looked in was a small, diluted black and tan heap of dog fur lying limply on a blanket. It was not the lovely black, rich brown, and white tri-color of most hounds and of my beloved Lauren. It was more like a dingy dish towel. I sniffed then wrinkled my nose. She stank. I knelt down next to her, noticing the pink bald spots on the black coat, and as I stroked, the limp lump glanced my way briefly, then cast her eyes back down. As I touched her she remained unresponsive. In her manner I saw not so much fear as resignation.

In order to postpone her scheduled euthanasia we needed to find her a home. Before Patty and I left, I asked the woman at the front desk not to euthanize her.

"We can't do that. If you knew how many . . ."

"What if I foster her?"

"Are you saying you will?"

"I think she is," Patty answered for me without looking at me, but gave me a sheepish smile afterward as we walked out the door.

Subsequent visits back to the SPCA to check on this motley scrap of beagle, revealed that while she had not been euthanized, she did have a severe case of mange and could not be taken to any home for at least a month for fear of spreading the condition.

But on January 27, I led a small, homely beagle out to the parking lot and into my truck to meet Flash. I was not adopting her but fostering her for beagle rescue. I knew she was too ugly for regular adoption, with pink and red sores around her face, ears, and anus. The hairless spot on her back was getting better, but her nose remained pink and freckled where the fur had not grown in. To add insult to injury, she ran on three legs. She had luxating patellas and would most likely need surgery. Not exactly the sort of dog about which one says, "Oh, I'll take her!" But I felt drawn to the little dog because of her pathetic appearance.

Perhaps the outcome of this story is all too obvious, for Chance hobbled into our household and into our hearts. She was not Lauren, but I saw that she needed me. Or, perhaps, the truth was that Flash and I needed her. Once again I saw that fate was not something for me to decide . . . my job was to trust. In time I would see that these humble companions taught me more about life than a shelf full of self-help books.

I led Chance slowly out into the parking lot. I thought she'd stretch or shake but she didn't. She walked slowly, stiffly, sniffing the outside ground for perhaps the first time in months. I hoisted her up into the cab of the old truck to meet Flash. He sniffed her. Her putrid smell may have bothered him, but if it did, I never knew. Gentleman that he was, he didn't turn away from her. Chance seemed resigned to her own fate, that of being taken away somewhere else, and she nosed Flash briefly then collapsed into a little ball of stinky beagle flesh right up against him. I got in the other side, glancing over at Flash.

"Everyone okay?"

Flash looked at me. Chance was asleep. I tried to read his face. More softly I said, "She needs your help, Flash. She needs love and care." And I swear he puffed out his dachshund chest and sat up tall. Or as tall as a dachshund can.

One day a few weeks after adopting Chance, I sat on the floor sorting through stacks of old magazines while mindlessly eating mini dark chocolate Dove bars. I would read the pithy little sayings written inside the foil then pop the chocolate into my mouth, trying to savor each one and make it last. Chance no longer smelled bad, and she and Flash were sleeping together in one dog bed like they'd known each other forever. I called Chance a beagle because she hunted like one and looked more like a beagle than anything else. But, with her tiny size and strange coloring, I think there might have been a pinch of Chihuahua in there somewhere too—although I never used the "C-word" around her. On this day Flash's head rested across Chance's back and their bodies spooned. I pulled back the foil on the Dove bar and read the following words: "Nothing is as strong as gentleness or as gentle as strength." I looked over to the dog bed, and Chance and Flash both opened their eyes and gazed back at me. I taped that candy wrapper to my fridge and it's still there.

It was only with the unexpected and initially unwanted arrival of scrawny Chance that Flash and I began to receive a glimpse of our intended journeys. Taking care of this severely depressed and malnourished dog (with whom I'd later develop the same intense bond I'd shared with Lauren) finally erased the last traces of grief from my heart. As she began to revive, shifting from the unresponsive and depressed dog we brought home into the joyous light she is today, so too did Flash and I reawaken with her, realizing we had been wanting all along to extend our small family of two.

CHAPTER 7

Ineluctable Life

The quieter you become, the more you can hear.
—BABA RAM DASS

WITH THE ADDITION OF CHANCE TO OUR FAMILY, A PERIOD of quiet well-being settled over our lives. There was a comfort like my morning cup of tea. Chance quickly emerged from her shell of sorrow, loving the attention Flash showered on her as he tried to mount her, perhaps reliving his pre-neutered days, and the two played and played. I realized that, however much Flash loved me or I loved him, he had needed another canine soul mate with whom to share the special thoughts that are unique to them, beyond the limits of my human mind. Perhaps because what animals understand is beyond the reaches of human thought, it is also beyond human articulation.

Just as I would never know Flash's full story—Ted's conjecture of shady drug deals notwithstanding—neither could I ever know Chance's background, although it was not hard to see her path before now had been paved with suffering. Often I would find her staring off into space with a look that went back in time. While at first I found her funny-looking at best and homely at worst, with her round head, bug eyes, and under-bite so unlike any beagle I'd ever known, in time I found her infinitely adorable. Perhaps true beauty is born of love. In any case, her stoic attitude was admirable, and together the two dogs, male and female, formed a happy unit.

Some people write in their journals to capture the moments that will never return. Some people write to capture those moments in hope of the promise of more. Some write only when the going is good, and some write most ferociously when life exposes the unbearable, as if this act of art could make sense of, if not mitigate, the horror. I tried to keep a steady hand at my journal through rosy and blue periods alike, but if there was an indication of joy for me it most likely lay in the camera. Walking through the pages of my photo albums, I traveled through time. Even after the digital age, numerous albums attested to this quiet, joyful period the three of us shared in our home that would often find me reading, gardening, editing, or just sitting outside while the two of them scoured the yard for rabbits, voles, and moles.

I suspect the camera's appeal had much to do with recording the small moments, intervals between the large moments of triumph and anguish, birth and death, where so much of real life resides. Or perhaps the allure was in preserving these peaceful times lest their quiet continuity be challenged later by contrary forces. An inevitability, some might say, when one lives long enough. But because I knew that the rush to find the camera took me from the very moment I strove to capture, I learned to severely discipline myself and choose life over record. In time, I learned simply to settle into the moment, letting it wash over me so that it would lodge in a corner of my soul somewhere many times more powerful in evoking memory in some far off year than on the chip of an electronic machine.

Nevertheless, around my house I placed these happy photos of Flash and Chance, mixing in photos of Lauren. But what were these compared to the life-and-blood beings who stretched and ran and grabbed for the toys by my feet? What were these beside the heavy breathing of those who slept by my side? Still, in the early stages, I was learning. With my photos fighting hard against impermanence, I had yet to find that lasting permanence through which we arrive by paradox. By letting go. I only knew that, for the moment, peace reigned and I wanted to hold on to it forever.

CHAPTER 8

Adventure

Great spirits have always encountered violent opposition from mediocre minds.

—ALBERT EINSTEIN

THIS PERIOD OF PEACE AND WELL-BEING PASSED OVER US quietly, covering us like a warm blanket protecting us from mishap, so that when I think back now, while I know we felt its ease, there are few distinct memories I can bring forth. Just a quiet sense of beauty. I know there are large gaps of life we lose, the day to day . . . and I don't know where this life goes. Some memories stay etched in the sand for long years thereafter, while others are washed away in the afternoon tide.

Perhaps it's the nature of humans to remember only the horrific or unusual. The majority of us lead lives of routine. Travel punctuates this uniformity with newness and difference, leaving memories sharper on foreign shores.

During the course of our lives together, Flash traveled to Paris and the south of France seven or eight times. He always wore a "service dog" emblem on his harness. This helped ease our way into places where he was forbidden such as, in supreme French logic, most Parisian parks.

I will digress here and say that as I aged, I learned to accept life in the package in which it came. Getting upset usually didn't help the situation. But there were still a few things over which I became distressed, one of which was industrial farming—in other words the large-scale suffering of billions of animals. Unless labeled as coming from a small, local farm, almost all the meat in the supermarkets is from factory farms, where animals suffer beyond what the average person can imagine, never knowing one good day of life. Then they're slaughtered. Animal testing was another area that caused me concern. Laboratory testing of human drugs or cosmetics on animals inflicts suffering on millions of animals with often faulty results. The problem remains: Animals are not genetically similar enough to humans to make them adequate test models, and yet they are emotionally similar enough to feel the same pain and suffer deeply.

On a smaller and more personal scale I found the fact that dogs were not allowed in many places that humans were somewhat annoying, for I knew most dogs to be better behaved than many people, not to mention filled with more heart. But rules were rules and as such, I learned to bend them gently if the bent rule did no harm to any person, animal, or place.

A neurologist wrote me a letter stating that I had a medical condition, and that my dogs could detect "an episode" before it occurred and bark to alert someone. There are trained dogs who do this but mine, in truth, did not possess this particular gift.

I will add that now, after working with a real service dog and writing her story, I see my error and would not again use the label on a dog who is not a trained service dog, for it gives a bad name to those dogs who've been scrupulously trained and whose life purpose is helping others. I was one of the few back in those early days; there was not the mass of people that there is today buying "Emotional Support Animal" badges and vests off the Internet for their animals. But if it is wrong for the masses then it wasn't right for me either, Kant's categorical imperative ever applicable. But in those early days, I knew no better.

One day in Paris, I stood with Flash and Chance outside a grocery store on the rue Mouffetard near my old apartment. Displayed prominently on their backs were the iron-on emblems I'd bought online. On each emblem, in black lettering upon white background, were the words *Service Dog*. A beautiful Parisian woman with ash blonde hair and an Hermès scarf walked up to us, squinting her eyes at the emblems. She looked at me and said rather quizzically, "*Ser*-veece dog."

I smiled.

"Service dog," she said again. "*C'est quoi ça?*" (What is that?)

"They are service dogs," I said in French, thinking quickly, not relishing the thought of a long discourse concerning my fictitious malady. The least said in that particular department, the better. You never knew when the karma gods would do a quick audit of your life. Instead I replied out of the blue, "They make sad people happy," and beamed back at the woman.

"Oh!" she said, her hand clasping at her heart. "I am sad." And to my astonishment, she explained to me how she had just lost her Yorkshire Terrier.

"I'm sorry," I said touching her arm. "Would you like for them to sing you a little song?"

Again her hand flew to her heart. "A song! Yes, tell them to sing me a little song."

I knelt down to where Flash was standing on the sidewalk and said in English this time, "Flash d'you want to sing?" Flash

42

began belting out the most melodious song and in no time at all there was quite a group of onlookers, standing and watching just like they did with the musicians, jugglers, fire-eaters, and mimes. And now a duo of singing service dogs. I thought Chance would sing if Flash did, but she did not chime in the way she usually did back home. Perhaps the commotion of the street overwhelmed her. I wasn't sure how Flash's song would be received; after all, Parisians demand much. But after Flash finished his song, the spectators clapped, and the sad French woman, who was perhaps now a little happier, thanked us profusely. *"Merci. Merci. C'est la verité. Ils donnent la joyeuse aux gens qui sont triste."* (Thank you. Thank you. It's the truth. They make sad people happy.)

"Au revoir," I said to her.

A kind Asian man smiled and nodded and threw pieces of ham to the little hounds. And Chance cashed in on Flash's performance without ever opening her mouth, except to eat the ham. But it was from that day forward that I would realize the truth of my words to the French woman: dogs could make sad people happy. Such is the strength of unconditional love, and I knew it was a two-way street.

I remember the first time I took Chance to Paris, I was blasé about it. Accustomed to traveling with Lauren and Flash, I'd forgotten the initial acclimatization period, not that either Lauren or Flash had ever needed much. I simply expected Chance to walk the history-laden streets of the city as if she always had. For the most part she did, perhaps picking up on my joy. But it was on our first trip over that, holding her on my lap as we rode the metro, I felt her shake. Maybe it was the jarring motion of the train as it rattled from side to side. Maybe it was all the foreign people crowding in around her with their funny odors and odd voices. Or maybe it was simply the newness of it all. I stroked her and spoke in soft tones, but her fear trembled up through my hands. What I witnessed next was a moment, insignificant to all but me and, in my human analysis, could be defined as selfless devotion, when Flash simply moved closer so that he could gently lay his head across Chance's shoulders. He didn't have to; he could have remained cradled in comfort against my stomach. Within seconds Chance's trembling subsided.

Another adventure occurred in Corolla, North Carolina. Here on the wide-open sands of a deserted winter beach, the hounds could be let loose. I was wary, but their love of running free overcame any anxiety. At home Chance, prone to follow her nose, was not let off leash as frequently as Flash. Flash, on the other hand, was much less apt to run off and was thereby granted the privilege of walking leashless. Yet he, too, was a hound and liked to hunt and roam. If I let him loose, I could usually call to him and he'd eventually come find me. But the cue that I was serious, if not a little angry, was when I'd yell out, "Flash, *right now!*" I saved this for only the most urgent situations.

At the beach, the dogs' love of running unfettered rubbed off on me, all of us feeling the freedom of the beach: the air and sky, the sea and the sand. My brother was with me then and together we walked slowly, removing socks and shoes even in the midst of winter to kick up surf and feel the cold sea wash against our feet, as the dogs raced ahead, sniffing, playing, rolling in dead fish. Ted had a dog and it was hard keeping an eye on all four dogs. Yet we had long before cultivated an element of trust—freedom for the dogs equaled joy for them, and therein too lay our own.

Before turning back to the house where we were staying, we paused to sit one more time on the cool, damp winter sand and feel the week's repose settle into us so that some patina of this calm would return with us to our workweeks and routines at home. The waves gently lapped closer and closer as the tide rose. I gazed out to the blue horizon, that boundless space where sea and sky connect and where, contained within, there waits something infinite. For as long as I can remember, I've been drawn to that spot where sea and sky converge. It fills me with both great calm and great uncertainty for that which lies beyond the knowable. I've heard it said that we have two natures, human and divine, and they depend upon one another for survival. Perhaps, then, we are both sky and sea, the point at which they forever merge and become one.

Behind me the dogs ran and Flash, wearing a red down coat to ward off the wind, dug a hole in the sand with earnest concentration. I stood then, waded into the frigid surf, my gaze on the rolling sea, the whitecapped waves, and the horizon beyond.

When Ted and I finally turned to head home, we called to the dogs. Mid-December winds blew sand into our faces, and the cold froze our fingers and feet, driving us back to the house.

It was when we were at the top of the long wooden flight of steps leading over the dunes that we paused to count dogs and realized we were without Flash. Thinking he was just under the wooden steps, I called, "Flash, come!" I waited and glanced around. Perhaps he'd scampered off to a neighboring house. I scanned the rows of beachfront houses behind the dunes expecting to see him sneaking around in his quest to scare cats or eat garbage. When I didn't see him I decided he must be off in the grasses happily hunting, oblivious to my calls or perhaps even out of earshot. The situation merited a *right now* and I yelled as loudly as I could, "Flash, *right now!*" expecting a small dachshund in a red down coat to materialize from under the wooden walk any second.

When no dachshund appeared I felt the first twinge of fear. Only then, when I turned around and looked back out over the long wide beach did I see him far below in his little red coat. He was in the spot where I had sat. He must have been busy digging in the dirt and had not seen us head home. He stared out as I had done, stared down the beach to where we had once walked. I looked at him far off in the distance and I realized but for the red coat he disliked I would have missed him. Then my legs were leaping down the steps two and three at a time and I was running down the beach. I called and called but the wind blocked my voice. Only when I was several feet from him did he turn and see me.

I saw the look on his face. I also saw the moment when it changed to recognition, relief, and then to joy. People who say animals don't feel emotions have obviously never lived with one—either that or they're highly unobservant. I scooped Flash up and as I held him against my chest, I felt his body shaking beneath the red coat and his little heart beating against my hand. Then together we walked back this way, annealing a connection that would fortify us in the years ahead.

CHAPTER 9

Sasha

Every life has a measure of sorrow. Sometimes it is this that awakens us.

—JACK KORNFIELD

WHEN THREE YEARS AFTER BRINGING CHANCE INTO OUR family I was about to rescue still another beagle with a history of appalling abuse, I knew I had to sit down with Flash and Chance and deliver my lecture on love.

"Having another dog in the house will not take away from the love I have for you," I said outside on the cool cut grass of a spring evening, looking back and forth between their dark questioning eyes. "You see, the way love works is that the more you give, the more it grows and the more you have." Perhaps speaking the words of my heart to them was not so much a way to convince them as it was a way to convince myself, for taking in another dog is not something one does lightly.

If the dogs didn't understand my literal words, they understood my intention and could feel my emotions. With them there had always been the absence of those small emotions—jealousy, irritation, self-righteousness—which so often accompany our human connections. For the dogs I felt only compassion, love, and respect. Whether they chose to love me in return was up to them, but was ultimately of little importance.

Love, like compassion, is limitless. If allowed, love always grows. Without love, we can't know compassion, for compassion is born of love, unlike sympathy, which includes pity. Indifference is antithetical to compassion. From its Latin roots *com*, meaning "together," and *pali*, meaning "to suffer," compassion by its very definition casts out apathy: "Sorrow for the suffering of others accompanied by an urge to help." We need not be in love with all who are suffering but we need to have felt love for someone or something in our lifetimes so that we may extend our love of one onto many. The Buddhists called it *maitri*, or "lovingkindness."

"This beagle needs our help," I continued. "She needs your love and acceptance as much as mine." Sasha had been chained to a tree on a grassless lot as the neighborhood children threw rocks and sticks at her. Sometimes they climbed up the tree and dumped down buckets of pebbles or paint or water onto her. The alcoholic father took out his anger and despair on her in a fashion I will not describe here. Helpless to flee her tormentors, she crouched lower and lower to the ground as though trying to enter an early grave.

Compassionate neighbors watched the horror until they could bear it no longer. They offered to buy Sasha for $20, liberating her from her prison temporarily, but they couldn't afford to keep her, and Sasha ended up, frightened and confused, in the local shelter.

Sometimes it's only in retrospect that we fully understand why someone enters or leaves our lives. I think Chance came to us because she had no thyroid function and needed to be medicated the rest of her life, something not everyone would have been willing to do. And Sasha, who remains timid to this day, forever casting her eyes upward in fear of sticks and stones from the sky, came to us, I think, because our home would offer her the quiet peace she needed. With this reasoning, we brought Sasha into our family.

When she arrived Sasha reminded me of Ferdinand the bull. Sweet, gentle, but fearful, she was often content just to sit and smell the flowers. "It is the sweet, simple things of life which are the real ones after all," wrote Laura Ingalls Wilder, and I liked to pretend she wrote the words to me . . . to remind me, if I lost my way, to always think like my dogs.

Chapter 10

Superman

Le bruit ne fait pas de bien. Et le bien ne fait pas de bruit. *(Noise does not do any good. And good does not make any noise.)*

—French proverb

At some point, though I'm not quite sure when or why, a friend of mine nicknamed Flash, "Flash Mon Do," which sounded very close to the French "Mon Dieu" or "My God," and that is how Flash became a deity. I wonder if it was ever that easy in ancient mythology. My brother, Ted, painted a picture of "the deity," further bolstering Flash's status. But he was not perceived as god by all.

Flash loved to leap from tall buildings, which meant in his worldview from furniture many times his height. He led the charge if visitors came to my door unannounced with never a thought that he was a tenth the size of whatever invader might be lurking outside banging at our door.

The most frequent unannounced visitors, for a period of time, were the missionaries. To understand the level of annoyance this could cause, it helps to understand the life of a writer, who, often in the midst of just the right sentence or thought can lose it with the most casual of distractions. Added to this was the fact that my Writing Room was a separate building about thirty yards from the house.

The room had wooden floors and brightly colored walls that I'd both stained and painted myself. There was one long, beautiful, rustic desk, bookshelves for my favorite books, and a woodstove for heat in the winter. It was spacious and uncluttered with a sofa on one side upon which the dogs could doze and gently sniff the breezes that floated into this safe sanctuary through open windows in the warm months. Conspicuously absent was a telephone, Internet connection, and any other discordant energy. My Writing Room had a warm, welcoming, and studious reserve, and I was instantly transformed upon entering it.

But this peace was shattered every time the missionaries came up my drive and knocked on the door to our house, at which point the dogs would jump from the Writing Room sofa, pop out the dog-door, and race the length of the yard back to the house, barking all the way as if their tails were on fire, and in through the second dog-door, scrambling and skidding over rugs to the front door where they would continue to bark and yip, thereby announcing the visitor. This meant that I now had to get up, leave the work I loved, and jog the same path as the dogs, except for the doggie-doors.

At first I was polite, accepting the biblical pamphlets they handed me, and even engaging in lighthearted discussions about Jesus. I knew they thought I was a heathen carrying god around in my heart, saying god was love—or worse, believing that he/she was all around us in the sky, in the clouds, in the trees, probably cavorting and mingling with fairies—instead of worshipping Him through dogmatic scripture or upon his narrow throne in provincial churches.

One day in mid-October the missionaries again descended upon our little world.

Knock, knock, knock, knock.

Yip, yip, yip, rep, rep, rep! The invaders are here! Come quickly! Flash raced out of the Writing Room up the yard to the house, in through the dog-door, and began leaping up and down at the front door to see through the glass and decide whether those outside the castle gates were friend or foe.

"*Coming . . . Hold on!*" Me, pen in mouth, glasses on head, hollering to the dogs to shut up, sending a toy rabbit sailing across the floor and startling Sasha.

"Hi! You having a good day?" Two women were standing there—one large black woman in a paisley print dress and one little white woman with a pinched face and eyes that darted all over but never once looked at me.

"Well . . . I . . ." I wasn't sure how to answer the question in light of the sudden intrusion.

"We just want to ask you if you're familiar with the Bible," the tall black woman said.

"Sure," I breathed. I was a bit out of shape and therefore out of breath.

"Well, we just wanted to read you a passage. Can we do that, read you a passage?"

"I guess . . . I was working . . ." I stood partially out holding the door open a crack but not enough so that Flash would charge out.

Rep, rep, rep!

"Flash, *hush.*"

"Do you read the Bible?"

"Well, uh . . . not every day . . . I have read . . ." I felt like I was being grilled in Sunday school and I kept thinking of the writing on my desk, the fire burning in the woodstove, the seasons changing outside the windows, the dogs nestled on the sofa as my fingers clicked over the keyboard, and how all that gave me structure and ritual and also deep peace. Standing there on my front porch, I suddenly realized my prior way of dealing with the evangelists was cowardly. I added, honestly, "But I've also read the Vedic texts, parts of the Talmud and Koran, and many other spiritual writings. I think Jesus would have wanted us to be open to other points of view."

You could have inserted a can of soup into the tall woman's mouth, it gaped so. No one spoke a word, so I continued.

"Lord knows, oops, excuse the unintentional pun, how much of his words are even in the Bible now. We just don't know. But I practice what I like to think are Jesus's original teachings," I finished.

A long pause and then, "You do? You mind telling us which ones you're familiar with?"

"Do unto others as you would have others do unto you," I said and wanted to add, and since I don't want others knocking on my door, pressing their beliefs on me, I don't press my beliefs onto others.

"Yes," the tall one answered. "We want to spread Jesus's word where His word is needed."

"I guess that means you think it's needed here?" I tried not to sound indignant, and wondered if I should point out my approach to Christianity with the birds out back.

Rep, rep, rep! But the discussion was starting to get to Flash. "*No*, Flash. I just don't think you should push your views on people already living his values . . . Jesus that is . . . not Flash. I . . ."

"We're not pushing our views. Because this is *His* word, not ours. And He wanted us to spread it and save as many people as we can. Those who believe and practice His word will go to heaven."

"Only Christians, in other words. See," I began, "that just doesn't make sense to me." I was about to ask her if there were dogs in heaven, but I decided that line of questioning wouldn't get me very far. "Don't you think that Jesus would not have wanted to exclude anyone who tried or wanted to be good?" I continued until Flash interrupted again—*rep, rep, rep*— somewhat more shrill and insistent this time.

"I think Flash must have a point to make." I laughed but no one was laughing with me. It was like telling a bad joke.

Rep, rep, rep! All at once Flash stopped barking and stared intently up at the two women. I wondered if the scriptures had anything about rodents in them. It probably wasn't the time to ask. But Flash persisted, perhaps urging me to have the guts to ask the question, so I said, "What do you all think about dachshunds?"

"Datsuns?"

"Dogs. Dogs in heaven?"

There was a protracted silence in which I heard the wind blowing through the leaves. A lone bird chirped. "We didn't come here today to tell jokes."

"Jokes? Oh, no, no," I laughed. "If I'd wanted to tell jokes this is definitely not the time to . . ."

The tall lady cut me off. "Jesus doesn't like blasphemers. Only Christians go to heaven. If you read the Bible and practice His word you can become a Christian. We do not exempt any individual. Jesus doesn't want you to become a Christian just because he was, but so you can save *yourself*."

And that finally got me. "Actually Jesus wasn't even a Christian, any more than the Buddha was a Buddhist or Krishna was a Hindu. Those religions were built up afterward. Jesus was a Jew. A Jew who taught what we think of today as Christian values. But he wasn't a Christian. He was a . . . carpenter."

Even though the sun shone, I felt a chill settle over my small front porch, like a light had been turned off and I wondered if I'd gone too far.

"Do you know that God is frowning upon you right now?"

"Is he?" I guess Flash Mon Do couldn't stand it any longer, and he pushed past me onto the front porch and began leaping up and down, snapping at the good disciples who were spreading the good word.

"Don't bite!" The little white lady finally opened her mouth to shout. It was the only thing I ever heard her utter.

"Go away! Go away!" the big lady yelled.

"Flash, *no!*" I called to him, but I was laughing as the women fled. I wondered if now was the time to tell them that "dog" spelled backward was "god." As their car rolled down the drive, Flash leapt down the front steps, flying along after it.

"Flash! *No!*" But Flash was so bent on his mission he didn't listen. The missionaries should have recruited him. I saw three big neighborhood dogs join with Flash in running off the intruders. Flash was leading the charge and the sight was both comical and moving. How it must have lifted his spirit. But I didn't want Flash running toward the road the way the roaming hounds often did. When he slowed I saw my chance and yelled, "Flash, *right now!*" And with that, Flash turned around.

When I saw him coming back to me, tail high in the air and crooked just a bit at the end, I smiled despite my momentary angst. Flash had accomplished in one minute what I had not managed in weeks. My god, *mon dieu*, my Flash Mon Do. If I was going to hell, I was going with those I loved and I was going laughing.

CHAPTER 11

Madonna and Dachshund

The bird of paradise alights only upon the hand that does not grasp.

—JOHN BERRY

IT WAS A WEEK AFTER THE DAY OF THE MISSIONARIES THAT I saw the painting of *The Madonna and Dachshund*. It just so happened that it was on October 27, which was Flash's birthday, or, since I would never really know his true birth date, the day I first saw him in Scotty's arms in front of the Barnes & Noble.

I was at my friends Tanya and Sasha's house. Tanya Anisimova is a renowned cellist who plays all over the world, from Moscow to Washington, but is unable to return to her native Chechnya for fear of being kidnapped. Her husband, Alexander Anufriev, or Sasha, is a Russian painter who also immigrated to the US and it was with his seemingly irreverent painting that I fell in love. Upon finding himself untouched after an earthquake destroyed everything around him, Alexander began talking to angels. Then painting them. Tanya once told me, "He only talks to dead people." But it wasn't true for he spoke to her, and he spoke to their two dachshunds, Hassan and Mouza. Flash, Ted, and I were regular visitors to their home, sitting down outside at their long table to the many-course Russian meals Tanya prepared, while the dachshunds played at our feet. She was that rare breed of accomplished artist who is also talented in areas outside of her specialty—well-rounded and gifted in "life."

On this particular day, Alexander motioned me to his studio.

"He has something to show you." Tanya translated his Russian and her beautiful voice floated through the small house like some KGB femme fatale in an old black-and-white film.

I walked through two rooms until I was standing in the bright, open studio where huge, elongated, Fra Angelico-meets-Fra Filippo Lippi angels stared down at me with benevolent expressions. Alexander spoke again, and I watched as he extended his hand out to something behind me. I turned, and found myself beholding a painting unlike any I'd ever seen—a painting I felt had surely been painted just for me. Cloaked in a flowing blue robe sat the Madonna, or perhaps she was just one of his serene-as-morning angels. In her lap lay not only the Christ child, but also a black and tan, smooth-coated dachshund. The dachshund was kissing the Christ child's face.

When I turned to Sasha he was grinning. He spoke to me while simultaneously puffing away at the short end of a cigarette, and Tanya walked over to translate, but this time I didn't need her explanation.

"He knew you would like it," she laughed. "Would you like a whiskey?"

"No, thank you," I said. But Sasha accepted one and blew smoke from his mouth.

I wanted the painting. Ted had always called Flash a deity, and Flash already had the divine nickname. I told them it was beautiful. I told them it was perfect. But I couldn't afford it just now. Maybe some other time.

Once home, I called the dogs outside. Because Flash's arrival day came at the end of October, one of the rituals we performed to celebrate was the tradition of planting bulbs, which we would watch break through the earth's surface in spring.

I bought packets of daffodils, crocuses, tulips, and hyacinths, and now I squatted in the shortened light of late October and began digging. I dug the first holes around the base of our old Honey Locust tree, which had saddened me when it died but whose trunk had now become a memorial of sorts to various flowers, prayer flags, hanging bells, and chimes. As I dug little holes and inserted each individual bulb, Flash walked up to me and studied my work.

He sniffed at each hole I'd dug. Then he too began to dig, his front feet working together as though one entity. I saw the bulb that I'd just carefully placed into the hole fly up and away from the earth.

"Flash!" I reprimanded. He stopped for a moment and turned to regard me, perhaps thinking I'd caught a mole. But when I proffered no mole, he was back digging through the dirt like he'd been commissioned to dig a pipeline, arching his back, jumping and jerking while his front feet dug, spraying dirt as well as the occasional bulb all over me. I watched dumbfounded, my hard work undone. Flash shoved his nose deep into the earth and Chance and Sasha walked over to us to see what was going on.

"Flash." I tried to sound stern. "You can help me. These are your birthday flowers after all. But you need to dig holes so we can put the bulbs *in*. Not unearth them." He was still digging, and paying not one ounce of heed to my instructions.

After a while he stopped and backed up to survey his work. I saw him look over at me, his long snout brown with dirt.

"I was digging too," I said defensively. "Just that all your activity made it somewhat distracting." Once again, I began to systematically dig a small hole with my trowel and drop in a bulb.

I think there is a satisfaction in seeing something you planted bloom, all the more so when your helper is a dachshund unearthing your hard work. And there is a special poignancy when you've endured the long winter months, and then, one day, feel the first soft air of spring. Flash sat on the ground beside me watching, and I smiled thinking how beautiful his flowers would be when they bloomed in the spring and how I would remember this moment. I didn't know then what lay ahead and I wonder if we could glimpse our futures, could we ever bear the present.

CHAPTER 12

The Beginning of Change

We who lived in concentration camps can remember men who walked through the huts comforting others, giving away their last piece of bread. They may have been few in number, but they offer sufficient proof that everything can be taken away from a man but one thing: the last of human freedoms—to choose one's attitude in any given set of circumstances, to choose one's own way.

—VIKTOR FRANKL

THE NEXT DAY IS THE DAY ON WHICH, WHEN I LOOK BACK, I realize our lives began to change. In hindsight, I see the shift was for my greater good, but at the time all that registered was pain.

I rose early. Out the window our yard was bathed in the golden-gray light that is as silent, yet different, from the silence of the dark. It is the sound and chill of just before dawn. Flash's cherry tree stood in the dusty light. It had never bloomed. I don't know why. I turned to the dogs in the bed and stroked each one. I noticed the flecks of white hair on Flash's chest mixing in with the black and brown. With the passing of the years he had picked up his share of gray hair, particularly around his muzzle and on his feet, but on this day, those gray hairs seemed more noticeable than ever. Over the years, my superman had also succumbed to bouts of back injury. I knew the signs well: no desire to hunt or even walk, a tense abdomen, a dejected look that appealed to me for help. With each flare-up he would stare up at me, entreating me to do something to ease his pain. And on this morning, Flash was exhibiting all the signs.

"What is it?" I asked. He looked back into my eyes and I could almost feel his pain enter my heart. I lifted him from the bed gently and cradled him in my arms. I knew the drill. Still holding him in my arms, I walked to the cabinet to retrieve the prednisone. I put half a pill in a little food ball and Chance and Sasha leapt off the bed and came running into the kitchen.

"Soon," I said to them. "Just wait a tiny bit." I held Flash and sang to him his special song. I knelt and stroked all the heads pushing into me for love.

The sun was just beginning to rise over the quiet mountain, fine fingers of light painting the tops of trees. I knew as it rose over the hushed fields beyond our house it would bring with it life and sound. I knew, too, within minutes Flash would begin to feel better.

But it was a double-edged sword. Prednisone is a steroid and, in those days, conventional treatment was what I opted for to ease his discomfort, while my own discomfort increased knowing that the steroids were not in his long-term best interest.

While on prednisone, Flash was full of energy and strength and therefore he was hard to keep still. Yet still I tried, which sometimes meant crating him. I am not a big advocate of crating dogs, although I do know that often, and especially if hurt, dogs may feel the security of a crate, in the same way they may seek out a cave in the wild. Many dogs are stoic in their pain because of an evolutionary trait going back to their ancestors. If a dog in the wild whimpers or cries when hurt, it's a dead giveaway to predators.

As Flash's back injuries became more frequent, I outfitted my house and yard with steps and ramps for him to walk up and down. Leading the way to the armchairs, the sofa, and the bed was an assortment of steps covered in brightly colored rugs and saddle blankets. When Amy saw them she rolled her eyes.

"Your house has really gone the way of the dogs." She shook her head, but in her face I saw the nod of approval. Because her home and life had long ago gone "the way of the dogs," for better or for worse, I think she was glad to find a convert to her way of thinking. My solution, however, would probably seem somewhat excessive to the general populace. Were the ramps a logical solution or no more than a step closer to eccentricity— the lady recluse with the hundred and nine cats? Yet I knew of several dachshund guardians who opted for ramps because a dachshund's back is simply not made for going up or down. It's rather a poor design really, working well only in the narrow, underground tunnels of badgers. I don't know what architect came up with the dachshund, probably some man or woman, years ago, intent on eating badger for dinner.

To me the steps were a better solution than back surgery. And it was the dogs' home as much as it was mine. Flash quickly learned to use the steps, and for a beat in time I could take a deep breath.

The problems came when he got excited, which was when he'd most likely jump. He avoided the steps then, preferring instead to sail off chairs or the big apple crate outside. I set up a long, gradual, carpeted ramp leading to the steep steps of the Writing Room, but too often he opted to hunch his back and hop up the steps instead of using his ramp. I knew frequent long-term steroid use was not healthy for a dog and I realized I had to find a solution. I decided to research alternative healing methods.

It was while I was looking into less toxic ways to help him that I had the strange sensation, like a feeling of thick fog all around me. Perhaps there's always a sense of unease when we're on the brink of change, like the snaking sense that comes when a person is deceiving us. I had been thinking for some time that I needed a change, but what, I didn't know.

Shortly after my flash of uneasy intuition, things began to spiral out of control for us.

CHAPTER 13

My Life

The real voyage of discovery consists not in seeking new landscapes, but in having new eyes.

—MARCEL PROUST

THE NEXT DAY I PULLED UP TO BASIC NECESSITIES WITH Flash in his crate. Ever since his bouts of back pain became more frequent, he came with me to work while the girls stayed home because I wouldn't leave a dog crated if I wasn't in the house.

I opened the passenger door and carried Flash at my side. My work at the wine bar included teaching courses to wine tasters about wine, making cappuccinos and cheese plates, and waiting on the occasional table. I think I made people happy and had enjoyed the simple job for many years, but I was realizing I needed to make sure I was making me happy too. I was thinking these thoughts, wondering if I should find new work, when I entered the shop.

Marie was in the kitchen but she came rushing out when she saw me full of frantic faux cheer and bad tidings. "Mrs. Fulbright came for her case of wine and it wasn't here. I had to give her two free bottles to calm her down! There's a bill in the office for $3,020 for the new insurance policy and we've only got $178 in the checkbook. Don't know what you want to do about it. But it's due now," she finished.

"Right."

"I'm gonna win the lottery."

"And then what?"

"Then I'll work here for free." She beamed at me.

"Any calls?" I asked and I knew that Marie understood I was referring to the city building inspector. We'd been told we might need a new septic tank in order to continue serving customers. The inspector had been supposed to call us days ago to let me know what we needed to do. Since it would cost a small fortune to dig a new one—Marie said we could put in a swimming pool for the same price—I'd been anxiously awaiting the answer.

"Yes, but none from our inspector friend," Marie answered breezily. Her advice to me on the matter was always the same: send love and light out into the world and don't worry so much. Even when our livelihood was at stake Marie was unshakable in her optimism.

I walked into the tiny office to find about fifteen or twenty messages written out to return.

The office used to be a bathroom. I could still see the spot under the desk where the toilet had once been attached. The walls were terra-cotta with green trim. I painted the shop to be reminiscent of the south of France, but many people who entered said, "Oh, it's just like Florida!" Or sometimes, "This feels like Santa Fe," which was more palatable. In front and in back of me were cork bulletin boards with notes, vendor numbers, and photographs of Lauren, Flash, Chance, and Sasha. Filing cabinets and my desk, also painted green, were crammed into the small room and there was barely enough space to squeeze in Flash's crate. Perhaps on this particular day, my thoughts said that cleaning and uncluttering my office would be a first step toward clearing and uncluttering my mind, and a first step toward change.

I hauled Flash's crate into the office where the smells from the kitchen wouldn't torment him as much. On prednisone he existed in a perpetual state of hunger. And while I might have wished to spoil him while he was injured by indulging his appetite, I did not. Keeping him svelte was imperative to his back's health. I had seen too many overweight dachshunds succumb to back trouble and sometimes paralysis. I was scrupulous with the three dogs' diet, picking greens from my garden in the summer and sautéing them together with humanely raised, free-range meats. Maybe we pass on to our children or, in the absence of children, to our animals those traits which are most important to us. I loved to eat good food, so it was no surprise that my three dogs ate better than many people around the world. Yet it was important to try not to value their lives above other animals, hence the free-range meats, which was an attempt, if feeble, to prevent the suffering of other animals for the benefit of my own three carnivores. Because I am also a pacifist, it was equally essential that they got along well, sharing not only beds, but also often licking clean the same plate.

The door to the office popped open and Marie stuck her face in to give me the once-over. She had long, naturally curly auburn hair, which she took great pains to straighten, blue-green eyes that saw straight to your soul. Even though Marie was Irish, she was like the Italian mother you never had, having grown up in New Jersey ("Joyzee" as she pronounced it). I often felt she could double for a Sicilian housewife.

"Change your thoughts. Be positive. We're gonna be fine. New tank or not," she said, needing only to glance once at my face.

"I wasn't thinking of the septic tank."

"Doesn't matter. Love and light," she reminded me.

"Love and light," I muttered. Marie was fifty-plus years old, the eldest of nine Irish Catholic kids, and everyone who walked through the doors of the shop loved her—with the exception of those who make misery a mission (which I guessed, judging from the tabloids and TV, included a fair number of people). Marie had been psychic since childhood and now customers regularly came in to ask about their futures and fortunes, or sometimes what their auras were registering. Customers liked and respected me; they listened to me, but they loved Marie, while the closest thing I had to unconditional love was lying in a crate by my feet.

"Why is it so easy to love him?"

"The *wiener dog?*" she sort of shrieked back at me. "Uh, like maybe because he doesn't talk back?"

"When asked why he loved his friend, Montaigne said, 'Because it was him; because it was I.' Whoever can explain love is far wiser than I."

"You think too much," Marie said waving her hands, the Joyzee spilling out. "Start thinking with your heart, not your head."

"I'll try."

"You're all heart. *Totally*. But you've walled it up."

"Each man sees what's inside his heart."

"You got that right at least. 'As a man is, so he sees.'"

"*Omnia bonus bona*," I said.

She cocked her head. "Okay you got me. Wha' zat mean?"

"All things are good to the good. That's you, Marie. You see good in everyone."

"And you do too, imbecile, or I wouldn't be wasting my time with you."

"Thank you," I conceded. My day was looking up.

She left the office, but when she returned thirty minutes later, the day went straight down the metaphorical toilet beneath my feet.

"May I talk to you in your spacious office for a sec?"

I nodded her in. She closed the door which got my attention.

"Alright, so . . ." She was staring into my eyes, not casting her glance elsewhere as people do when delivering unpleasant news . . . or telling lies.

I looked back at her, waiting. Beyond the closed office door I could hear snippets of conversation from a couple arguing and critiquing my Italian wine selection.

"Quite limited selection . . ." Pedantic male voice.

". . . what about Lambrusco, sweetie. . . ." Pleading female voice.

". . . not *serious* wine . . . too sweet . . . now Barolo or Barberesco . . ."

". . . you're sweet and I . . ."

". . . sorry-ass collection of wine. . . ."

Then Marie spoke, saving me from lecturing Mr. Barolo on the art of compassionate critiquing. "Sweetie, I'm not sure if I should say anything because it might not even be true. But I just heard a rumor . . . about the building inspector. People are saying he's looking to shut down some of the smaller restaurants in town. Some kind of 'crackdown' on 'substandard establishments.' Basically, quirky little places like ours that don't conform to regulations like the chains do. Rumor has it, we're next to go."

As children, Amy and I had gone swimming out in the ocean off the Outer Banks. I both loved and feared the huge, crashing waves and hung on to my blow-up raft as I crested each one. I remember the feeling of my stomach rising up into my heart, and the same feeling came to me now. I sat without speaking for a moment. Then, softly, wanting to believe my words, I said, "We'll be okay. It's just a rumor."

"Exactly," beamed Marie. "We just need to stay positive. We'll dig a thousand new septic tanks if we have to!"

I smiled weakly, my "brave face" not convincing her one bit. I knew Marie could tell I was scared of what would happen if we lost our business. She saw through me just as I saw through Flash when he put on a brave act for my benefit. She bent to hug me, then left me alone.

When the door shut, I sat very still. I felt terrible for wishing earlier for a change of job. All of the sudden I loved the little restaurant I'd created. I loved it with a fierce devotion and determination for it to go on.

On the wall before me Lauren's liquid brown eyes stared back into mine, but they were forever frozen on a two-dimensional photograph that had begun to curl up at the edges. Then I looked down and saw two quiet brown eyes gazing up at me . . . very much alive and real. In his eyes there was not so much entreaty as there was a softness whose provenance could only be love. It was all around me then as if I had just been bathed in the most tender emotion known to man. I leapt from the chair and crouched down, my bottom bumping against the wall. I stared back at him through the square metal grid of the crate door. I watched his whiskers and lips puff and quiver as he let out a silent cry, the pain naked in his eyes. Then he was quiet and we were speaking to each other with a language that knows no barriers of time, space, or species. A language used from one generation to the next, one culture to the next, one heart to the next, and I knew that if Flash were in another continent I could still reach him.

At last I spoke aloud. "I'm so sorry. Don't worry, Flash. I'm going to make you feel better. I love you. Please don't worry. It will all work out."

Chapter 14

Catalysts

When all is done and said, in the end / thus shall you find, / He most of all doth bathe in bliss that / hath a quiet mind.

—Lord Thomas Vaux

The next morning I stood before the mirror brushing my teeth with the special fluoride-free toothpaste I'd bought after reading that fluoride was not in fact the childhood friend with whom we all thought we'd grown up, but an imposter, sort of like when you read in the newspaper thirty years later that your first grade boyfriend turned out to be a serial killer.

In order to quiet my thoughts, I'd practice mindfulness. I didn't realize how out-of-control my thoughts were until I went in search of my glasses which I'd set down somewhere with as much mindfulness as an Alzheimer's patient.

"Where the . . .?" And then my thoughts would get into it: *So this is what you call mindfulness?*

"Screw off," I said back. Welcome to my state of mind.

I sat down in the armchair to begin my morning meditation, breathing in, quieting my thoughts, breathing out, releasing all negativity. *How can he just shut us down when we've tried so hard?* I tried to envision a different outcome, but I couldn't rid myself of images of the little place I'd worked to build crashing down around me.

When I arrived at the shop with Flash in his crate, Marie met me at the door.

"Hello, Miss Bearer of Bad News and Tidings," I said, walking back to the office without stopping, and setting Flash on the ground so I could slip out of my coat.

"Sorry I told you," she answered following me.

"It's okay. I'm just tired. Tired of being misunderstood by everybody."

"All great men and women are misunderstood. Look at Jesus," Marie persisted, and all I could think of was the missionaries handing out pamphlets on my front doorstep.

"Right, and where'd it get him? Thank you, but that particular outcome's not calling to me right now."

"But he's more loved now than anyone else," she attempted.

"I'm not so sure about that . . . and anyway, I just want one person to love me. Not half the world."

"I think you may be safe there."

I smiled at her then.

"Just go into your heart," she said looking at me. "There are your answers. They may not be anyone else's. But stick with what you know is true for you."

"Like Socrates," I said. "He died for his beliefs."

"Like I said, all great men and women are misunderstood."

"Jesus and Gandhi and Buddha and Martin Luther King and Albert Schweitzer and St. Francis took on the problems of the world and threatened the status quo . . . that's why they were misunderstood."

"You're still in good company. And you're still ahead of your time." Then anticipating her next words, I mouthed simultaneously as she began to speak, "Send love."

But when she walked out the door leaving Flash and me alone, I put my head down onto the desk. *Send love.* I would need to practice. I didn't want anyone asking me, "What are you thinking about?" only to receive in reply, "Oh, I was just thinking whether poisoning the building inspector would be looked on more favorably by the jury than an accidental boating incident."

Six hours later I stood before twenty wine tasters on the cozy back porch as the gas fire warmed the October air. Sunlight streamed into the back room past the funny bunched up curtains I'd bought in Provence. I tried to see its warmth as an offering of hope, but instead I felt hollow, insubstantial, and only half there. My mood altered the character of the friendly, familiar room and gave to the wine tasters an unreal significance and stark strangeness. Normally these people were like family to me. I loved them and, while most were retired and older than I was, I called them all "my kids." None of them had any idea that this place we all loved would soon be history. I tried to focus on their faces. I tried to focus on what I was doing. As I poured the wine I explained how the red clay soil of Bordeaux's right bank was more conducive to growing the merlot grape that thrives there, while the left bank with its gravely soil was better for Cabernet Sauvignon. The banks were so named because, just like the Seine in Paris, the Gironde estuary separates the two sides, and if you stand on the river facing the direction in which the water flows, the left is on your left and the right to your right respectively. But I saw that most of the wine tasters were more concerned with catching up on local gossip. As I tasted through each of the five wines, telling anecdotes, stooping only occasionally to tell bad jokes to rouse their attention, my class became tipsier and the noise level rose. One woman, a guest, seemed genuinely interested, and met my eyes each time I looked at her.

An hour and a half later, I rushed into the steamy warmth of the office to check on Flash. But when I carried him outside and set him onto the ground to piddle, his back end sunk to a sitting position. When I urged him forward to walk, he would not. I propped up his haunches with my hand, willing him to stand, but when I let go, he collapsed.

The wine tasters began trickling out.

"Oh, isn't she sweet?" A hand reached over to touch him.

"He," I corrected. I was used to people thinking he was a female, attributing the error to his sensitive energy.

"He doesn't make a peep. He's so good." It was the woman who had listened attentively.

"Yes, he is good," I answered, thinking to myself, especially since right now he must be in pain.

"Is everything alright?" she asked looking into my eyes.

I nodded but looked away.

She explained that we had a friend in common. "She said you'd be receptive to my work. I do healings with electrically charged essences. It's a total body analysis and we use kinesiology to determine imbalances." I listened to her as she explained to me the work of Dr. Reuben T. DeHaan and told me of a young boy with cancer she'd treated. "If ever you need it . . . or someone you know. . . ." And she handed me her card. It read: *Susie Hoffman.*

"Thanks," I answered, only partially taking in her words. The air was bright and cold and when she walked to her car, I saw the autumn sun hovering above the mountains about to drop below.

I put Flash onto the front seat and set the crate in the back of the car.

"Going home," I said to him and he pricked his ears and tipped his head, perhaps pleased with the prospect of seeing Chance and Sasha, or maybe of eating his dinner.

"How fine you are," I said to him. "How fine and how brave." On the way home, I pulled up to my mailbox to retrieve the mail and saw Nora walking down the road. I was tired and didn't want to take the time to chat, but she walked over, her face smiling at me and warming my heart.

"Hey, Kay, hey. How's it going?" she asked.

My face must have spoken in answer, because her white teeth disappeared and her eyes bore into mine. "You alright?"

"I'm okay. I'm worried about little Flash here," I said, pointing to him on the seat. When she asked what the problem was, I explained as quickly as I could. Outside my car windows the light was slowly fading. I saw a lone bird fly across the gray sky.

"Have faith, honey. Just have faith. Ask for a sign and one will surely come when you need it the most. Just have faith."

"Thanks."

Faith. There was that word again. Maybe that was my problem. I hadn't had enough faith growing up.

At home Chance and Sasha greeted us at the door with great displays of tail-wagging and toy-shaking, and I tried to feel their easy joy. How I'd missed them. Sasha jumped up and placed her front paws on me, her ears flapping out like an airplane, and Chance darted through the house, squeaking her toy in a primal, inchoate language, a language we four shared. The house was small but there was always warmth and love and peace.

I put Flash in the dog bed before the woodstove and told the girls to be careful around him. Tentative October light, the last of the day, came in through the big window, settling on his back. I watched Chance licking his ears, gently and methodically, as Flash lay beside her with closed eyes. I grabbed the phone. Only then, with the help of family and a few friends, did I make the decision I'd been afraid to make on my own. I called the Veterinary Referral Center and scheduled an appointment for Flash to have back surgery. The Veterinary Referral Center was more than two hours away, which meant that the girls and I would have to stay in a hotel while Flash had his surgery. I didn't know then that I was about to embark on a journey that would break open my heart and leave behind the prison that had contained my soul.

When I hung up I knelt beside the dog bed in the early evening light, surrounded by the three little hounds. Flash gazed up at me with bright eyes. He wanted dinner.

CHAPTER 15

Crisis

The world breaks everyone . . . but some of us become strong at the broken places.

—ERNEST HEMINGWAY

IT WAS FIVE A.M. ON NOVEMBER 2. I DROVE EAST WITH FLASH in the front seat. He lay in his bag gazing at me as Chance and Sasha slept in the backseat, which was outfitted with a large futon cushion. I felt pure love for these three canine souls whose welfare lay largely in my hands. There was the daily routine of filling bowls every morning and every evening. There were the walks through wind or cold in the fading light when I returned home tired, ready to rest, but knew the dogs were anxious to be out. . . . They inspired in me a selfless love—the small acts of caring for another without any desire to be loved in return—and I found this love more satisfying than all other kinds, romantic attachments included.

My day began with caring for the dogs, birds, and plants, and it was there that it ended too. In between lay all the small moments of being, moments that ran together and were quickly forgotten in a day's time, but moments that made up our lives nonetheless.

In return for this care I was filled with something that would remain unmarked by the rifts and gaps of human connections and disappointments: a love, as limitless as the sky, based not on conditions, but existing for its own sake. And if the dogs didn't verbally thank me—nor did I seek it from them—they told me with expressions of joy: a soft look in the eyes, ears flattened back, wagging tails, exuberant leaps, and play bows. They thanked me just by being there.

But in between there also fell the larger moments that would not be soon forgotten. Moments of trauma or sickness like the one we were presently experiencing. I looked at Flash's small and delicate body, which seemed insignificant beside everything in this great world, except to me.

I felt like a fly sheet covered in stress. My mind raced. Was I doing the right thing? Would Flash survive the surgery? I'd known dogs who'd gone under anesthesia for mere dental work and had never risen to see the next hour of daylight. Flash's surgery would last several hours and would be complicated. Would he be one of the ones who didn't wake up? Or, if he did awaken, how long would it take him to recover? Was I making him suffer needlessly? But he already was suffering. Maybe I should have called to have him euthanized instead. But no! He was nowhere near ready to die.

I turned and let my eyes rest upon him. He lay in his mesh travel bag sleeping with a lip puffed up, revealing his exaggerated overbite and exposing the few teeth he had left. When other dachshund lovers walked up to us, they always made nearly identical comments: "He has a very long nose." Spoken slowly, carefully, never cruelly—simply an observation. Or sometimes it was, "I've never seen one with . . . such a long snout." Once, a girl sat up at the shop's front counter and held him in her lap. She had short, black painted nails, black dyed hair, torn clothes, and silver studs through her nose and lower lip. She studied his face then turned to me and stated, "He has such a *refined* nose. I want a dog with a refined nose like his." And I've always remembered her kind words, so at odds with her harsh, gothic appearance.

In the car, Flash could sense each time I turned to look at him. He opened both eyes to gaze back at me with quiet trust as if it were he who was reassuring me. Did he know I was memorizing each gray hair mixed into his black coat, or marveling at the left ear that always lay crimped?

When we arrived, I left Chance and Sasha in the car with the windows cracked and hoisted Flash in the bag up over my shoulder, pausing before walking up to the veterinary hospital to look into his dark eyes once more.

Then we walked in.

It was a plain brick building. The place had changed a little since the last time I'd been. There was a new wing and new receptionists, but it retained a strange familiarity, born from the time I had spent there with both Lauren and more recently Chance. I watched the activity of the receptionists behind the counter. To every person walking in with a beloved animal, this was potentially a difficult experience, but to these girls behind the desk it was everyday work. A woman ahead of me stood shifting her weight from side to side. I could feel her nervousness, or perhaps it was my own. She had no dog. Maybe she was picking up her companion.

When the receptionist found my records she looked up at me eagerly.

"You're client number 316," she said, smiling.

I waited for her to tell me I'd won a stuffed animal or free lunch at Wendy's, but when I didn't answer she explained that I had been one of the practice's first clients—there were now more than forty-two thousand. I thought back to Lauren for a moment, to them no more than "client 316," then to Chance who had spent nine incredibly difficult days and nights here, after a double copperhead bite less than a year after I'd adopted her. She had probably funded the new wing. She became their number one priority and I was not given encouragement that she would live. Day after day the internal bleeding continued, her blood oozing from every orifice. But I wouldn't give up on her and, after three blood transfusions, one plasma transfusion, heartfelt prayers from those who cared, and an outstanding doctor, Dr. Charlotte Davies, Chance was alive and outside waiting for me in the car.

I took a deep breath, trying to believe that life works itself out in the end . . . in just the way it's meant to. I could smile in gratitude at the fact that Chance had survived despite my inscrutable fears. But how would this day go? I needed to apply the same calm knowing to Flash. But I couldn't. I felt an odd, unfamiliar fear. I tried to eschew it, for I knew of too many people who had become hostages to fear, paving a path to illness and despair.

Flash was more sensitive than Lauren or Chance. He didn't have the toughness or reserve they did. And although he was not as fearful as Sasha, I knew that behind his brash barking lay insecurity. He poked his nose up from the bag and I touched the top of his head. Finally we were led to an examination room to wait some more.

I thought about Nora's words. Have faith. I had read somewhere that waiting is an act of faith. If I thought at all about faith, I guess I'd say I had faith that Flash would make it through the operation. I had visualized him together with the girls at home afterward, yet the odd sense of something being not quite right persisted. I stroked his swollen body. The room smelled stale and sterile. I turned and saw the lowered blinds covering the window, blocking out the day beyond. Light. We needed light, and not the artificial kind. I moved to the window and opened the blinds. Soft light spilled into the room through the opened blinds, soothing and kind like a hand offering hope.

Outside was a white pine tree next to a sugar maple. I thought of Lauren, our little pine at home; I took it as a good omen. Fallen red leaves lay scattered around both trees on the patchy brown grass. Birds hopped from one limb of the pine to the next. An ordinary day. People were driving to work, running errands, seeing doctors. I held Flash up to the window to regard the scene. And together we stood in a moment so pure, there was no space for fear, only love that began with quiet understanding and pushed away worry for those passing seconds.

I kissed his face. "I'm so proud of you," I said. What did he know of what was about to happen? I stroked his back. "And I love you so much. . . . *I love you*." Overused and worn, those three short words, and yet with their utterance I felt a current between us. Love is silent, but love was speaking to me louder than words, and I was only just beginning to understand. Flash turned his head away from the window and the still life beyond and looked up at me.

When the doctor walked in she looked about sixteen. Yet her competent, if clinical, attitude reassured me. Then I was handing Flash over to her and stepping away from the room. Flash was looking back at me from her arms, and I wished I knew a way to step back into time. I walked outside and breathed in the air, so different from the air of the hospital.

A few yards ahead I saw two pairs of beagle eyes peering at me, drawing my attention away from what I'd left behind. When I opened the door, the girls jumped from the car and ran across the same brown grass that Flash and I had moments ago observed from inside. The past caught up with me, then dissolved, and I found myself standing in uncharted territory. I stamped my feet to center myself, but found within only hollow ground. I turned to face the back facade of the animal hospital; beyond those walls was Flash. Then kneeling down, I called to the girls, who sniffed their way over to me, and one touch was enough. I squeezed my eyes shut.

We drove toward Richmond and checked into the Homestead Suites, the only place I could find that allowed dogs. I was tired and ready to collapse on an impersonal bed, but I listened as the receptionist told me story after story about a Chihuahua-terrier—or "terrorist" as she said—that she had almost euthanized for behavior problems.

"Now he's in boot camp!" She laughed.

"Thank you for taking the time with him. Thank you for not euthanizing him," I said.

"Oh, I wouldn't have really! But, well, maybe I would have. . . ." She laughed guiltily.

"So many just need a chance. So many are misunderstood." I hoped my calm voice would not expose my alarm.

"Aren't we all!" She laughed again and I sensed that she had a part of her life about which she didn't talk. Because I listened to her talk about her problem dog, she only charged me for one dog, not two. I didn't talk to her about Flash. I didn't tell her he was in surgery. I didn't even mention his name. And as I stood there, I felt the odd superstition of omitting his existence as if that might portend our life ahead.

She handed me a key to room 217.

It was a room like hundreds of others. Nondescript, sterile, ordinary, but a room that became unique unto us. To Chance and Sasha the room was pregnant with scent and full of life. They trotted to the corners of the room, divining the secret pleasures and pains of previous guests. On the bed they pranced and danced and rubbed their faces into the patterned bedspread. Across from us stood a tall mirror, and I caught myself looking into it without seeing. We had a sink, a fridge, a coffeemaker, and a microwave. In different circumstances, I too would have felt the excitement that a new hotel room offered.

I realized Flash was at that very moment undergoing his myelogram. The room was too dark, and I snapped the leashes back on to the girls and set out to explore. I could send Flash healing thoughts from my heart, but it was best not to dwell in the possibility of human error or complication. After walking around a suburban concrete shopping center that gave Sasha a fright, we returned to the hotel, to the bed and my books, to a world of shallow comforts. I put the cell phone next to my bed and thus began our wait.

I had with me a photograph of Flash, a poignant face shot my brother took. I stared at it and Flash gazed back into my eyes. The photo captured the essence of his sensitive soul, and I thought that if I could remain looking into his eyes until the call came that he was out of surgery, all would be okay. I cuddled up with Chance and Sasha on the bed and stroked them while looking at Flash's photo, trying to connect with him the way my friend Amelia Kinkade, psychic and author, had taught me to do when Chance and I visited. Using Chance as her demo dog, she told her animal communication class, "To connect, you need to quiet your thoughts and drop your attention down into your heart. From the loving space of your heart, you build a bridge of loving energy." Once the class focused on their hearts and not their heads, Amelia instructed them to send beams of light from their human hearts to the animals. In order to telepath with another being, she explained, you need an open heart and stable emotions, unclouded by personal grievances, desires, or agendas. Unclouded by grief or stress.

An hour passed. No phone call. Then two hours. Then three. Four hours passed, long after the estimated time the doctor had given me. There was nothing to reassure me that Flash's surgery was finished and he was waking up.

In those days I carried a dumb phone. When I realized I hadn't left the phone on, I breathed in relief. Until I saw that there were three voicemail messages.

I played the first one. "Ms. Pfaltz? This is Dr. Luster calling. We need to talk to you about Flash. Please call us right away."

I felt my heart beating. The brain will try to deny, but the heart *knows*. I erased the message and played the second one. "Ms. Pfaltz? This is Dr. Luster again. We're trying to reach you. Please call us back immediately. I need to talk to you about Flash."

I did not bother to erase the message this time. Neither did I listen to the third message. I dialed the clinic. "I'm returning a message from Dr. Luster about my dachshund, Flash," I said to the receptionist. As I paced room 217, Chance and Sasha followed me with their dark eyes from their perch upon the bed.

"Okay. Hold on and I'll see if she's available."

"Life changes in the instant," Joan Didion wrote. "The ordinary instant." Chance and Sasha lay on the bed in identical positions, with heads lowered between their front paws, watching me. I knew they could sense my shift in energy and I spoke softly to them while I waited for the doctor. But anxiety coated the room like hot, humid air and my thoughts churned . . . the intuition I'd been stupid to ignore, the strange knowing I'd tried to push away, building within me and turning to something heavy and damp like stone when the doctor finally came on the line.

"Hello, Dr. Luster speaking."

"Hi, Dr. Luster, it's Kay."

"I tried to call you several times." Her solemnity was not lost on me.

"I know . . . Flash . . . ?"

"We called because based on the radiographic and myelographic appearance of the thirteenth thoracic vertebrae and the spinal cord through this lesion, Flash does not have intervertebral disk disease, but rather most likely a primary neoplasia of the vertebrae and spinal cord in this region. There's about a one to three percent chance of this when we go in for back surgery. We could've done a biopsy while he was under, but when I couldn't reach you. . . ."

"He's alive . . . ?"

"He's waking up now."

I felt a wave of relief wash over me. Then I pronounced her word, "Neoplasia?"

"Yes."

"Is it . . . ?"

"It could be a secondary neoplasia, in which case the cancer could be anywhere and is probably quite advanced. Or more likely it could be a primary tumor, but the chance of metastasis is very strong. Particularly to the lungs."

She continued talking while I stood looking at Chance and Sasha, and it was one of those moments when all things converge. I tried to match the doctor's practical, matter-of-fact tone and not let my voice waver when I asked, "Neoplasia means cancer?"

"A tumor, yes."

I looked at the soft brown eyes of Chance and Sasha watching me, listening, while Dr. Luster continued, explaining the disease the way she probably had to many others before me.

"Unfortunately, for vertebral neoplasia, especially neoplasia involving the whole vertebrae as seen in this case, with the extension into the spinal canal, surgical removal is not an option for treatment or cure. A biopsy would be required for a definitive diagnosis of the tumor type. This would involve invasive surgery to collect this sample, although possibly decompression of his spine through the area of the tumor could also be performed. There would be significant risk of causing complete paralysis with this option, from which he may or may not recover, and little hope of a long-term effect. There would also be the risk of destabilizing his vertebral column with more invasive decompressive surgery."

"Is there nothing . . . ?"

"Other treatment options, including chemotherapy and radiation therapy, are also of minimal efficacy. Typically, palliative treatment is pursued, with humane euthanasia once signs progress to the point where they cannot be controlled with medication."

There was a silent moment before I could form the next words, words that would shape our future.

"How long does he . . . ?"

"We're looking at no more than two or three weeks. Three weeks at the very most."

CHAPTER 16

Grief

Give sorrow words: the grief that does not speak/ Whispers the o'er-fraught heart and bids it break.
—*MACBETH*, ACT IV, SCENE III

A CHILD MIGHT SURF THE WAVES FOR HOURS ON END, DODGING the giant crushers, coasting to shore on others, but there usually comes a wave that will topple him over, tossing him beneath the ocean's powerful weight for a moment of terrifying clarity. He sputters to the surface, gasping for air. Only later do the tears come.

I knew Dr. Luster could hear the grief struggling for release in my voice, and I wondered if she cared.

"When can I pick him up?" I asked, wanting more than anything else to be with Flash.

"If he's had no seizures from the myelogram by this evening, you may be able to bring him home."

"Is there . . . is there nothing . . . I mean, price would be no object. Is there no way he could live longer than two or three . . ."

"I wish I had better news, but with this kind of tumor, the size and nature of it, I would be wrong to offer you any hope."

"Nothing . . . ?" I said, and I heard the impotence of that one word as though it was stuck in my throat.

"It would take a miracle."

"Thank you," I managed.

"I'm sorry. I wish I had better news," she said once more.

I wondered again how many times she had to deliver the difficult words to anxious animal guardians, how often had she spoken words that could cause such a strong physical reaction in the listener's body. In the large mirror I saw my face, creased in grief like the wife who has just become a war widow, or the parent who has lost a child . . . everyone, I suppose, at some point.

When I hung up the phone I grabbed Flash's photo, wanting to become possessed by that distinct and separate time. An awareness of absurdity for any past sense of unhappiness washed over me then. I realized that I had been happy—even in the midst of my work drama. But I could only now know that happiness in the abstract and in relation to the news I'd just received. The quiet comfort of our house, the joy of watching the seasons come and go, of watching three healthy dogs, the absence of pain—all had been ours. But all that was untouchable against this.

I lay face down on the comforter and cried. God, why does anybody take in an animal and love him? It hurts too much to love anything this much. Finally I spoke quietly to the girls. "I'm sorry. It's Flash . . . Flash has . . ." But I was unable to finish explaining to them what I think they already knew, perhaps had known all along. I stared at his beautiful photo and his eyes looking back into mine, as if this moment I was experiencing had been forged long ago in another timeless universe.

I reached for the phone again and called Ted. When I explained the details to him, I thought I heard a catch in his voice. Whether he grieved because he knew I did, or because he loved that little dog, I wasn't sure. I tried my mother and father but answering machines were the only response and somehow, "Flash has a tumor. He has two weeks to live," was not something in my power to leave on a mechanical machine.

When I called my sister I could no longer control my faltering voice. It was Amy who had given me Lauren, and it was Amy who gave me Flash.

"He's alive," I said quietly. I spoke softly but quickly so my battered voice wouldn't scare her. "But . . ." I began again, and as I explained to her the diagnosis, I tried to mimic the doctor's cool reserve.

"At least he's there," Amy said. "And he didn't die under anesthesia. Focus on that for the moment. He's with you still. You can spoil him and love him for these few . . ." She didn't finish.

"Two or three weeks . . . what does that mean? Do you have any idea how time has just radically changed for me?"

"Some idea," she answered. "But there's always a . . ."

"Don't say 'silver lining.'"

"Okay. But you have to live in the moment now more than ever. The future's never a good option."

"Yeah, but anything but this."

"No yeah-buts. There's only now."

"I just need to see him. I just need to be with him now."

"I know. Hey . . . keep passing open windows." She brought out the words which we had written to each other across continents for so many years when the going got tough. It was a line from a John Irving book, and the heroine had to "keep passing open windows" and not jump out.

"Promise," I said to her. "Love you."

"Love you too." We hung up.

Three weeks. At *most*. Maybe not even. All at once it meant everything and nothing. The ultimate, meaningless riddle of time.

I called the veterinary hospital three more times, but Flash was still under observation. I lay back on the bed between the girls and they leaned into me, nuzzling me, sniffing me, sometimes scratching an ear or elbow.

At dusk, we stepped outside. Beyond the parking lot, the trees stood in silence, and the air was still. I loaded the girls into the car and we drove to Whole Foods just as the sun was beginning to balance over the tops of bare trees, leaving a yellow glow. It was the hour that ends the day.

In the vast store, I walked in a daze, carrying a basket past the orange, red, and green vegetables imported from countries far away, past the teas purporting to cure every possible ailment, past the organic shade-grown coffee and raw kombucha, past the olive bar and the cheese station, past the chocolate towers and freshly baked breads, and past the guacamole, hummus, and baba ghanoush. I wondered how many of the people who rushed by me pushing carts of expensive food had heartaches too. How many others, crossing paths with mine for one fleeting moment, smiled through their tears? How many had a spouse who'd walked out on them, or a mother in the hospital? Or a vet who had just told them that their dog was dying and nothing could be done?

I was standing in the checkout line when a woman two rows over began arguing with the cashier in a shrill and angry voice. The man in front of me wore an overcoat with the collar turned up as though fighting bad weather. He was speaking softly to our checkout girl. Then he turned, looked into my eyes, and said, "There is so little love in the world."

I stared at him dumbly. Back in the hotel I dipped chips into a plastic container of guacamole and worked my way through part of a pound of mixed olives.

"Hold on," I said to Sasha, who I sometimes believed saw me as no more than a food dispenser. "I'm going to feed you. I've got something special." I felt guilty for feeding Chance and Sasha a treat without Flash. I also felt guilty for choosing their life over the life of an intelligent fish or for feeding them wild-caught coho salmon which cost more than many third-world workers made in a month. But we ate, and as we did, I felt the comfort that food has brought from time immemorial.

Then there came a shadowed hour where, without distraction, the sense of grief pervaded, sticking to me like a second skin. The three of us were quiet. More than quiet . . . we were still. There was a sense of waiting and a sense of something lost.

Yet he was not lost to us yet! My heart screamed through the silence. But the vet's words had cast their spell, and like a small atoll whose reefs erode with each passing storm, I felt my world washing away.

Sometime after eight o'clock, exhausted from emotion, I drove through the darkness to pick up Flash. The roads were dim and I was glad. In the darkness I felt hidden from the harsh world of normal lives. Chance and Sasha lay solemnly behind me, aware of my discordant energy and uncertain how to help except to offer their quiet presence.

Two stanzas from Tennyson had found their way, how I didn't know, into my scattered consciousness:

Behold, we know not anything;
I can but trust that good shall fall
At last—far off—at last, to all,
And every winter change to spring.

So runs my dream: but what am I?
An infant crying in the night:
An infant crying for the light:
And with no language but a cry.

From past experience I knew that even our darkest nights give way to dawn, and every winter turns to spring, but in that moment, following a sea of red lights, I didn't see how hope was possible.

I thought about my fears driving up that morning, another world away, and again I thought how I had fretted about the surgery and anesthesia. Why do we ever worry when the outcome is somehow, somewhere, already known? *Maktub,* as the Arabs say, "It is written." Had it already, long ago, been written? In quantum physics they say that we can, by observing something differently, change the outcome. The observer effect, it's called. I began to believe that had I just had a few more positive thoughts concerning Flash, none of this nightmare would now be happening.

But when the tech walked up to me with Flash wrapped in a towel, I let go of all the stress of wondering what I could have done differently and felt only gratitude for his warm and living body. Relief combined with a love so vast, it had no beginning or end. He was here. She handed him to me and said that while he hadn't experienced any seizures after the myelogram, I must still be vigilant. "As if," I wanted to say, but never mind.

How many other people had returned to collect their animal companions only to receive the accompanying news that frightened them? No one offered me sympathy. The techs can't, for they'd burn out if they got emotionally involved with each case. I took Flash from the girl and pressed him against my breast for the second time on that endless day. She reached her hands around under him and showed me how I would need to express his bladder. He could neither stand nor urinate on his own. I noticed he held his head straight up in the air. Was it a reaction from the procedure or had he twisted something in his spine?

"He should be back to normal by tomorrow," the tech stated, and I could see from her harried manner she was exhausted.

As I stepped from the hospital out into the cold night air, I clasped him against my chest.

"You're here," I said softly looking at my dog. He looked up at me with a straight neck. His back was shaved in a long reverse Mohawk stripe about three inches wide and seven inches long down his spine. I touched it and stroked him, wanting to tell him "It's okay." But I had never lied to any of my dogs; they could always tell.

When I set him on the grass, he fell over and didn't walk again that night. I lifted him to my breast once more and carried him toward the two pairs of eyes staring out, waiting for us.

In the car I slipped Michael Jones's *Dream of the World* into the CD player and kissed Flash's face. Mixed into the tears there was gratitude. Somehow, behind the sorrow was the lightest brush of joy. He was back where he belonged, and for that moment I didn't think about the future.

Back at the hotel, drained and depleted, I was ready to sleep beside the three dogs, now that our family was again complete. Even though I knew I would sleep the deep sleep of the depressed, I welcomed the proximity and time with them all. The thought and possibility of losing Flash under anesthesia had made even this small comfort a moment to cherish. I arranged Flash in the bed up by my pillow so I would hear him should he begin to seize, and pulled a towel under him to prepare for incontinence. But it was only after I'd undressed and brushed my teeth that I began to understand his pain. He would not or could not put his head down, and held it straight pointing toward the ceiling as though in a brace. He had been breathing hard, but when I stepped from the bathroom he was whimpering, and raspy coughs escaped from his long nose and mouth. The stress of it hit me harder than the sorrow, for with sorrow there is a purity that can cleanse. But stress only gnaws away at your soul, casting out goodness, creating ugliness and despair. I knew what we had to do.

I dressed and once more slipped harnesses on Sasha and Chance and gathered Flash into my arms. It was late, nearing midnight, yet still we found ourselves surrounded by other people driving to other destinations. The white headlights and red taillights moved steadily beside and before me and were oddly comforting as we drove back to the vet's.

Before being discharged, Flash had not been given any painkillers and, while not an overzealous proponent of conventional drugs, I was not going to let my dog suffer when a shot of morphine would give him a respite from pain and the night's rest he needed. I carried him in and waited while the techs took him wrapped in his towel to the back. Although my new fear had not been vanquished, I did at least feel gratitude knowing that this time Flash was not going back for surgery, but would in fact return to me in minutes, relieved of some of his pain.

I watched people walk in with dogs by their sides even at this hour. Some were trying unsuccessfully to check on patients behind the closed doors. Some came with emergencies. I heard a screech of tires outside. Several heads turned to peer out into the dark as if any diversion was better than the waiting.

I sat quietly, but when the thick glass door burst open, letting in a draft of night air, I turned to the sound of a long cry entering with the outside air.

"*Somebody! Pleeeze, help!*"

My tired eyes beheld a woman about my age with a feral look to her face, and unruly, matted hair, carrying a small white dog who draped across her arms without moving. The little fluff of dog was not bloodied, but there was no mistaking his or her broken condition. It was not so much the absence of movement as it was a certain angle of limbs. The woman rushed to the front desk.

"*I need the doctor now,*" she pleaded as two receptionists emerged from behind closed doors.

I rose as she spoke in sharp, broken sentences and explained the accident that had befallen her Josie. Then there was a moment when the receptionists ran back to find a doctor, any doctor, and the woman and her broken dog were left standing in the center of the lobby. I had the desire to console her, to lay my hand on the little body we both knew might not last the night, but I became self-conscious of the other people in the waiting area. I was relieved when a tech ushered the woman and dog through a door to the back.

The sense of my own impotence merged with the greater sense of life's random events and the helpless dog whose life I would never know. As I sat back down, I realized that from the moment the woman and her dog had entered the hospital, I had not thought about Flash and my own problems. I vowed I would never again stand dumbly by, watching without offering comfort when comfort was needed . . . and so easily extended. I vowed I would help in whatever way I could—a kind word or hug—regardless of how self-conscious I felt, whenever someone was in need. I made the promise to myself and I made it to Flash.

I remembered Marie's words: "Send a loving thought." The means to be happy is within us every moment, even in the midst of crisis. All we have to do is send a loving thought.

Forty minutes slipped by in which my mind was occupied with these and other thoughts. The woman with the white dog did not return, and I wondered if she'd been given a special seat somewhere close to her dog. When the tech returned with Flash, I asked why he was holding his neck straight, but she couldn't answer. When I expressed worry that he was still paralyzed and incontinent, she said that he should improve by morning. Somehow, in comparison to the little white dog, these effects now seemed diminished. I asked after the fate of the white dog and again she said she did not know.

I staggered back to room 217 with my bewildered little crew and undressed for the second time that night, then slipped into bed beside Flash, while Chance and Sasha, already asleep, pressed up against him, perhaps to comfort him, or perhaps to ensure that he not be taken away again. I grabbed another towel, and only after settling down with the faint smell of dog pee in my nose did I feel any peace as I gazed into his face and stroked his back and awkward neck. But he wouldn't look back at me.

"What can I do? How can I help you?" His breathing was strained, and he could only groan.

The desire to cry and have someone comfort me in my sorrow was strong, but there was no one. I continued stroking his neck and back.

"Do you know how much I love you?" I rubbed his tummy and massaged his funny dachshund feet. I pulled lightly on his ears and covered his nose with kisses. "Chance and Sasha love you too. You have so much love in your life. You always will. Promise."

When we find ourselves in a place of darkness it seems there has never been any light. I was the child in winter who cannot perceive of summer's golden, lazy days. I stared into his face, trying to remember those summer evenings when he would be content to hunt the path of a long vanished mole, and I would be content to sit and watch the light change as the three of them pursued their simple joys. If it's true there isn't any time, then this moment was all that existed, and the possibility of a different outcome seemed beyond our reach. But after a dazed and ragged time that seemed to have no substance, I watched as the morphine began its narcotic magic and Flash relaxed, his deep breaths becoming light snores until his head and neck mercifully dropped. Finally he slept. And only then, did I.

CHAPTER 17

Turning toward the Light

Lighthouses don't go running all over looking for boats to save; they just stand there shining.

—ANNE LAMOTT

A FOG HAD SETTLED SOMETIME DURING THE NIGHT, AND IN the day just beginning there was a cold dampness. I stepped outside with Flash in my arms and the girls on their leashes. Birds already active. Sun still behind the horizon. And Flash still paralyzed. When I set him on the ground, his hind end collapsed.

"Hey, it's alright, little man. It's alright," I soothed and scooped him up again, holding him close. We walked out into the parking lot, Chance tugging on her leash to sniff and explore each bush, corner, and foreign dog's mark, and Sasha, nervous and wary, jumping and shying away from noise and human approach. I put Flash on a patch of loamy mulch, and again he toppled over. When I tried pushing his bladder to express the urine, he turned to look at me beseeching with reproach. I saw sad eyes looking up at me, the whites showing below his irises, not above, like when he sang to us with zeal. A motorist roared past us much too fast and I jerked the girls toward me while crouching next to Flash. I felt the life we had shared was slipping to some dusty corner of earth beyond my grasp, beyond even my imagination, as though the peace and harmony we'd known so well had vanished from our world, never to come back again except in memory.

Then, without turning, I could feel the moment the sun rose above the tree line. An early jet was moving across the sky in takeoff and I saw patches of blue tearing holes through the fog. I hugged Flash and slowly turned so that, for one instant, we were momentarily blinded by the sun's light. And for those fleeting seconds as I held on to him and clasped the two leashes, we were bathed not only in light, but in that quiet acceptance which seems to lull even the fiercest of storms. And all was very still.

Then there came a moment that has remained with me ever since. Was it a dream or did it actually transpire? So often the dreamworld carries more tenor than the so-called waking reality, yet I knew I had not been sleeping; there is a different feel to subconscious thought. Or, if I had been asleep, I was now fully awake. And in this awakened state, I not only said this aloud to the three dogs, but also felt it deep within me: "This death sentence does not have to be our future. We can tap into the power of miracles." I knew the ability to heal lay within us all. Yet too often we accept what others tell us as truth, and don't trust ourselves. We turn to others outside ourselves for help, and believe only doctors and conventional medicine can heal.

The man in Whole Foods had said there was so little love in the world, but who can understand what goes on in an individual heart and, standing there in the asphalt parking lot, somehow, I knew this love was all around us.

Perhaps, in retrospect, it was in that short, unreal space of time that I felt my first sense of hope, for often it's in the midst of our darkest despair that we find the first taste of serenity. Even if I wouldn't admit it or speak it aloud, ever since Dr. Luster had given me the shocking diagnosis, I had already jumped ahead to a time when Flash would not be with us. Had I not discussed with Amy the feeling of control that euthanasia allowed? Letting Lauren die in my arms, surrounded by great love, in the quiet peace of our own home had brought me comfort and, with time, the ability to move forward, happy for the memories we'd shared. Amy agreed that at least this way I could make sure Flash was at peace. The idea wasn't so bad considering Flash was thirteen, considering the alternatives, and considering they always leave us too soon. In this way I could savor a bittersweet poignancy of the hallowed days that were to follow; I could live each hallowed day to its fullest, the way we should do with all our days, yet somehow never seem to do until something shakes the ground beneath the legs we always felt were steadfast. This way I could spoil him for a month then be by his side for the very last time, staying with him until the moment when he would have to continue the journey alone.

The moment in the morning sun in the parking lot, while ephemeral in its spreading warmth, nevertheless extended itself subtly into the following days, pervading what might have become weeks of debilitating despair. For it was driving home, Flash in his bag beside me, head pointing up but not quite as stiff as earlier, Chance and Sasha in the back, that I began— mile by mile, breath by guarded breath—to expect the miracle that had stirred within us earlier. Perhaps it had been when I turned, holding Flash, and we four headed into the light. Perhaps it was the power of love as I drove silently looking at him with his shaved back lying beside me, vulnerable, yet accepting.

And with the feeling came a lightness. The heavy grief we'd felt in the hotel room was lifted and I felt buoyant. If only for a few miles. Then the worry and stress began again, but they would, as the parade of miraculous days marched by one by one, never be quite as intense. Something else was guiding us now.

CHAPTER 18

Finding a Cure

Let nothing disturb you, / Nothing frighten you— / All things pass, / But God never changes.
—Sainte Thérèse d'Ávila

Once home I tried to resurrect the moment in the parking lot, but I kept sinking into the grief that comes from the fear of losing what we love. Whether our bond is with a person, animal, or a way of life to which we've grown accustomed, the fear of loss is strong. Yet every single one of us must say good-bye to every single one we know. Either we leave them or they leave us. No one is exempted from that singular sorrow. Yet out of that comes life's greatest beauty, or as Rumi expressed it: "The rose's rarest essence lives within the thorn."

But, once home, I longed to go back to a time before this time, when I had not realized our lives existed in small patches of sunlight . . . full if simple lives, free from illness. I felt a hungry absorption to study and memorize every contour of Flash's odd body, every black or brown or gray hair. The spongy pads on his feet. His toenails. And his face. There was the black gumdrop of his nose, his long muzzle, his forehead and expressive umlaut. And now his dark eyes clouded with worry.

Flash was for me both a loved one and a way of life, but overriding my fear of loss was the pain of watching him suffer. I remembered from Lauren how much grief felt like fear. After the doctor's words and my initial shock, there came the difficult days of trying to figure out what to do, caring for him in his paralyzed state, expressing his bladder and cleaning up poop.

With many questions jostling through my mind and no answers at hand, I sat down before the computer, hoping my stay there would be brief. But there in the virtual world where I was not at home, I found massive amounts of information, confusing to me and often contradictory. I knew many of the treatments worked, but I also knew not to go crazy and bombard Flash with seventeen different kinds of Chinese herbs or homeopathic remedies at once. There was skullcap and pau d'arco, *Viscum album* (mistletoe), and *Artemisia annua*, which was actually wormwood. An old bottle of absinthe I'd bought in France sat high on a kitchen shelf. It was the real stuff, made from wormwood, and now I wondered about the kind of despair depicted in Toulouse-Lautrec paintings that drove people to an existence fueled by absinthe.

There was curcumin and quercetin. There was green tea, blue green algae, and ginger. There were numerous mushrooms: maitake and reishi. There was spirulina and chorella, iodine, magnesium, lipoic acid, and folic acid. There were all kinds of blends of herbs and pills, liquids and powders. There was fish oil and vitamins E and C, and selenium and sea salt and zinc and perhaps most of all: whole, fresh, real food. Cancer loves sugar and carbohydrates, so the ideal diet in treating cancer is a high-fat diet. But in time this would pose problems for Flash's heart, so good protein and good fat was what I opted to feed. No canned food. No kibble. Certainly no grains or processed carbs.

I fed the dogs only organic meats and vegetables from local farmers and supplemented Flash's diet with some traditional Chinese herbs.

I ordered Jason Winters tea, a tea reputed to heal cancer, and various supplements from a holistic website, and was taking copious notes from other sites when it hit me: I was spending these precious moments before a rectangular screen, when I belonged with Flash. Intuition told me that it was my love and proximity that would prove more effective in Flash's healing than Chinese herbs and vitamins. I rose from my desk and lay down beside him in a patch of sunlight in the living room, where I began to stroke him and sing softly without asking him to sing back.

In the afternoon, a thick bank of clouds piled up over the mountains. I walked outside and stood under the viburnum. In the spring, its spicy scent was my favorite smell of all. How I loved the big, white blossoms and yet how ephemeral was their life. Now, many of its dark, red leaves had fallen. All at once I dropped to the ground, my shoulders heaving. How could I endure the spring if he was gone? I remained there in the yard on all fours until Chance walked up to me. "I'm okay," I said, wiping my nose. "Just fine." But she didn't believe me. She looked away from me and yawned.

Back inside I lifted Flash to my face looking into his eyes and planted a kiss on his long parsnip of a nose. "How're you doing?"

He stared back at me with dull eyes.

"Flash, d'you want to *sing*?" No, he didn't want to sing. I placed him into his bag, slung it over my shoulder, and, giving cookies to the girls, I said good-bye to them and drove with Flash to the shop.

CHAPTER 19

Empathy

Love alone is capable of uniting living beings in such a way as to complete and fulfill them, for it alone takes them and joins them by what is deepest in themselves.
—PIERRE TEILHARD DE CHARDIN

WHEN I ARRIVED AT THE SHOP, I WAS UNPREPARED FOR THE warmth and love I felt when I saw Marie, as well as a seemingly endless array of customers to whom she'd explained, against my vague wishes, about Flash's diagnosis.

Then came another moment like the one in the parking lot, except this time the visions were real, not spectral ghosts from past and future. Through the doors walked two young musicians in their twenties: Lindsey and Sally Rose. They played for us on the weekends, filling the back porch where our customers dined, not only with their songs but also with their vibrant youth. But I saw at once that all was far from vibrant and good. Sally Rose's face was red and splotchy. Lindsey had an arm around her, guiding her in the direction of the coffee station. I had a momentary, not entirely irrational, thought that the reassuring warmth of coffee would right whatever wrongs had occurred. As I followed them with my eyes, I remembered my vow to Flash the night of the white dog. I walked over to the two girls.

"Hey."

"Hey, how's it going?" Lindsey replied in her gentle, laconic style.

"Can I do anything to help?"

"*Oh, Kay,*" Sally Rose threw her arms around me and cried into my neck. How easy it was to feel another's pain, but how hard it was to take it away. I'd heard somewhere that when your fear touches someone else's pain it becomes pity, but when your love touches someone's pain it becomes compassion.

As Sally Rose told me about a man she was dating who was exploiting her generosity, I realized that it was precisely her open and loving nature toward everyone that had gotten her in the muddles she was consistently getting into.

She spoke and cried, then spoke some more, and I thought of my own problems. I saw the golden edge to my own anguish, for it was what allowed me to better understand Sally Rose. I thought of Flash. To be human means you have to go through various stages of growth—you can't skip or miss any of them. I spoke to her from my heart, knowing that one day her sadness would pass and she'd see this time of grieving as having strengthened her loving character.

I wanted to tell her how much I respected her. I wanted to tell her how much wiser and more aware she was than I was at her age. I wanted to say, "He doesn't deserve you. You're far too good for him." Or, "You're young. All this will pass." But I said nothing and let her talk through her tears. I stood listening as she cried and spoke. Finally I said, "I'm so sorry, sweet Sally Rose. I love you."

"*Oh, Kay,*" she said again. "You always help me feel better. *I love you so much!*" I hoped her effusive displays of love wouldn't hurt her, but I also hoped she wouldn't lose that spark of life as she grew up, letting the disappointments of adulthood blunt her spirit. I was thinking ahead to a future that held a happy Sally Rose in its arms, when I realized that what had just passed between the two of us was more real than a future that might not happen. I vowed I would call her later that evening and tell her that one day she'd look back on all this as a time of growth and be grateful.

No sooner had Lindsey and Sally Rose left than my friend Gayle walked through the door and the conversation turned to dogs and inevitably to Flash, who was still in his bag by my side. I'm not sure who comforted whom the most. I felt strongest when he was slung over my shoulder, my arm around the bag. He watched the customers come and go, but there was none of the usual animation in his face.

"I'm sorry to hear about the little man," Gayle said, extending a hand out for him to sniff. "You remember Newt? He was diagnosed with a tumor on his liver and given one month to live. That was a year ago, and a couple of bottles of bloodroot later."

"Bloodroot?" I questioned.

"*Sanguinaria canadensis.* Bloodroot or black salve or neoplasene was used extensively by the medicine men and women of some Native American tribes, who also used it as a paint for their bodies and a dye for their clothes. Newt takes it orally since his tumor's internal, so I guess Flash would too. But you can also apply it topically."

"I never heard of it."

"Apparently the bloodroot recognizes which cells are cancerous and goes about destroying them. The salve is used topically to treat and disintegrate melanomas and sarcomas, and used orally to treat internal cancers. It can also be injected but in some cases it proves too caustic and animals have anaphylactic reactions."

"You don't know what this means to me."

There is a relief, akin to great joy, that is only felt in opposition to pain. I wondered if this might be one of pain's purposes in life: to awaken in each of us our deepest sense of joy and gratitude. I hugged Gayle.

My next step was to find a vet who was familiar with bloodroot. The closest one, Dr. Crowley, was in North Carolina, another state away.

Flash comes
home to live
with me. He
seemed
so small.

Flash chasing
the flash.

Flash off the coast of
Villefranche, France,
in the bag he'd
later use when sick.
"Flash-in-the-bag,"
as Ted called it.

Flash enters my heart.

"Sing, Flash! Sing!"

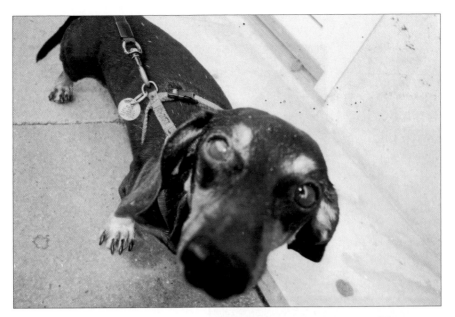

Hello, Flash! Ted took this picture on the streets of Paris.

Chance, Sasha, and Flash atop the old apple crate. Flash loved to survey the fields beyond our house from the height and safety of my arms.

Beseeching
me with one
crimped ear.

In the crate
with pain in his
eyes.

Eating without
the use of his hind
legs. His crate sits
beside him.

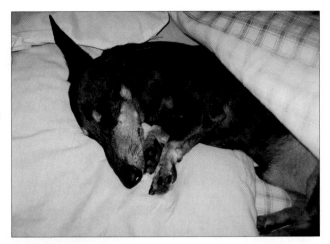

Flash asleep with his nose not quite twisted to the side.

The Madonna and Dachshund by Alexander Anufriev.

Flash, Christmas morning. The only present I wanted was long, low, and black—and wearing a red bow.

The dog bed in front of the woodstove was the favorite winter spot.

Flash sees the flowers bloom. This was the photo Ted took of Flash beside the first crocuses of spring.

Flash in the flowers (and weeds) of spring.

Flash digs in the dirt after our session with Rebecca and after I'd given him steroids. The rectangular shaved strip on his back is still visible.

Sasha, Chance, and Flash in the backyard with the viburnum in full bloom and the Writing Room in the background.

The picture I took the day before Flash died. He looked handsome and alert, but the creases between his eyes spoke of confusion, and with the lined agitation, I sensed he was not the Flash I had known for thirteen years.

Sasha and Chance.

CHAPTER 20

The Journey Begins

Flow with whatever may happen and let your mind be free. Stay centered by accepting whatever you are doing. This is the ultimate.

—ZHUANGZI

ONCE AGAIN WE ROSE BEFORE DAWN, BUT THIS TIME I TOOK only Flash. We'd be back well before evening, and Sasha and Chance could stay at home.

It was an overcast day in late autumn, the kind of day that intensifies the color pigments in the trees. The light was changing day by day, bringing to us that shortened, inward season of winter. But for now many leaves still remained and the roadside was a blaze of color. With Flash in the bag on the passenger seat beside me, and hope ablaze in my heart, we set forth on another journey together.

I thought about the pure space my grief had dug. Sorrow breaks open our hearts, making room for love, and in that moment we live in the pure space of the present, caring for our sick or dying loved ones with a consciousness largely absent in the routine days of happier times. In this way the days turn sacred, and therein lies the miracle. We live in a sacred space that is bearable, even beautiful, until it's shattered by death. For

109

a while afterward, the holy space stays with us, perhaps through shock, but the expanse is short-lived and the grief of the physical loss sets in. I remembered this all too well from Lauren and wanted to do it differently with Flash. I wanted to be present in my heart for the entire journey, and grateful for every part of it.

As I drove with Flash beside me, I observed my thoughts. I found images painted with fear's brush passing through my mind only occasionally, and I wondered why only life and death events had the power to subdue the mind's chatter and insistence on trivial things.

I remembered the outpouring of compassion around the world after 9/11, and how people stepped out of their usual roles with openness and love in their hearts to help others, casting aside fear and prejudice. People everywhere opened their hearts to neighbors and strangers alike, to people of other races and cultures and forgot, for that brief moment, the differences, seeing instead our many similarities. But all too soon, the collective heart began contracting, the small thinking returned—suspicion, mistrust, and hatred were more rampant than before. Why is it we have to be teetering on the edge to let go of petty grievances? And why does it so often seem to require the death of someone we love? Where would the world be today had we been able to stay in that space of caring and love after those towers fell?

I turned to Flash. I didn't know how many days or hours I had left with him. As we drove through a corridor of trees, squares of warm sunlight drifted across his back and moved on. The sun rose higher. The skies grew brighter and the day changed shaped, taking on a fragile poignancy that would soon mean death for the departing season.

We sped past a shop with hundreds of cement statues outside and I had an urge to look for St. Francis of Assisi, the guardian of all animals. I noted the next road so that perhaps we might stop on our return. The sign read 888, three times infinity, and eight was my favorite number. At this point I was willing to take anything as an auspicious sign. Even a street sign.

CHAPTER 21

Realization

As a man's real power grows and his knowledge widens, ever the way he can follow grows narrower: Until at last he chooses nothing, but does only and wholly what he must do.

—URSULA K. LE GUIN

WE PULLED INTO A SMALL, UNASSUMING VET CLINIC. I checked in with the rather brusque receptionist; when she asked questions, I felt like I was being interrogated. She had brown eyes and short reddish hair that flopped back and forth as she snapped her head up and down, sipping from a white paper coffee cup with lipstick stains on the front. When I asked her opinion about the bloodroot she said she had no idea.

I filled out the appropriate forms then sat down with Flash to wait. It was not the first time we had waited and I would come to learn much from the gentle and accepting, albeit frightened, presence beside me. The receptionist glanced at him but didn't speak. Behind us was a large hand-painted mural of a tree, its branches reaching out. I regarded it absently, before seeing that, there, hidden in the brown trunk and paint, all number of animal faces peeked out. I wondered how many people missed seeing those funny faces. I looked down, and another face was peering up at me with trust.

I stroked him and saw behind the dark eyes the worried, nervous expression that spoke of the very emotions he tried so hard to hide. Another veterinary hospital. More procedures which were scary and often painful. I leaned over and kissed his eyes where I always did, whispering, "Oh, Flash, my Flash. You are so fine. So very fine." But his nervous agitation spread to me and I stood, hoisting the bag to my shoulder, and walked over to the glass door to stare out. The light was muted.

"Don't leave now," the receptionist said without taking her eyes from her paperwork.

"Oh," I turned to her. "We're not. Just wishing we were."

"Tell me about it," she said and looked up at us then. "I have a sick child at home." I moved away from the light and walked over to her. "But I came in to work."

I nodded, somehow grateful she was here to help us. "I hope he . . . ?"

"Yes."

"I hope he gets better."

I saw her brown eyes soften then. "Thank you. I can't think about anything but him."

"I understand."

"Do you? I keep thinking that every person who walks in here will be able to see through me and see I'm . . . that I'm a nervous wreck," she finished.

"They're mostly worried about their own problems. They . . . we . . . don't see."

"I resented coming in this morning," she said and looked up at me quickly, like she had said she'd mugged someone in the alley before coming into work.

"It doesn't show." I smiled at her, thinking perhaps that was her greater fear. "You don't look like a nervous wreck either."

She smiled back at me. "I think it did show before." She took a deep breath. "I feel just a little bit better now."

"I hope he heals soon," I said again and returned to the tree mural. Flash stared at the tree. Maybe he saw rodents lurking in its branches.

In the next instant we were summoned by the doctor and walking back to another sterile room with the same models of various stages of dental decay, the same posters of the flea's life cycle, the same beige tile flooring. And there was the same fear in Flash's thin face. Yet, in spite of his fear, I tried to hope. But the news was not good.

"I think he'd make a good candidate," Dr. Crowley said, leaning forward, his bushy eyebrows giving him an air of gentle tolerance combined with knowledge, his low voice coalescing with hope in that small room. Then the eyebrows rose upward. "The more difficult piece is that your Flash is on prednisone. The steroid gives him some mobility and allows him quality of life."

"Yes."

"The bloodroot and the prednisone are counter-indicative. The prednisone reduces the swelling caused by the tumor."

"Right."

"Thereby giving him relief from pain and the ability to walk."

"Yes."

"But you see, the bloodroot will seek out the tumor and initially cause great swelling, but eventually . . . we would hope, perhaps as soon as within two or three weeks, it should begin to shrink it."

Again, I felt the feelings of helplessness that I'd experienced when the young doctor pronounced Flash's life expectancy.

We didn't have two or three weeks in which to experiment. "In other words, the bloodroot could cure Flash of the cancer completely?" I asked.

"Correct. I have an 80 percent success rate with this."

I nodded, wondering about the other 20 percent.

"The prednisone only treats the symptoms," he continued. "And is extremely harsh on his kidneys, and liver, while also lowering his immune system—the very last thing you want to do with a diagnosis of cancer." I knew all this and disliked giving the steroid to Flash, but the relief it gave him was essential. Over and over I had to remind myself that with a prognosis of three weeks at most to live, we were opting for quality, not quantity.

"Cats and humans can take prednisone long term, but dogs experience too much stress on the kidneys, and once a dog has kidney failure it's a quick and gruesome road to death."

Once again there was the inner anguish of decisions that were mine to make for another. Another whom I loved. Should I keep him on steroids, thereby reducing his pain, cherishing each day, each moment, knowing that he was comfortable while knowing that the cancer was growing inside him and I was limiting his days? Or should I try to extend his life with the bloodroot, which offered really the only hope of beating the cancer? It seemed an obvious choice if what I say I wanted was true—quality of life for him over quantity.

Dr. Crowley had an 80 percent success rate with it, but he also had only seen nine cases. I would have felt a lot happier had he had such a success rate with nine thousand cases. But I kept thinking of Newt, Gayle's dog; I kept thinking of one month turning to one year with the help of the bloodroot. If I could just have that time. . . . As I sat in the room, listening to the difficult news while holding Flash in my arms, I felt my mind already forming a decision from which I'd find it hard to turn back. My desire to beat the disease and see Flash live was too strong. I told the doctor I was going home to think about my options, but in my heart I knew I was going to order a bottle of bloodroot.

I remembered a philosopher who spoke of the agony of indecision, the hardest part the deciding. Once the decision is made, we simply do it, but until then there lay so many questions under so many unturned stones.

With Flash slung over my shoulder in the green mesh bag, I walked outside and was about to step into the car, when I realize I should let Flash urinate. I carried him to the end of the parking lot where three tall oaks stood. I slipped him from the bag and he staggered a few steps then fell over. He struggled upright and stumbled off to a spot to sniff. I watched him closely, feeling my heart thump with each faltering step he took.

When he raised a tentative hind leg, I tilted my head to where the tall oaks stood. Behind their curled, brown leaves I could see the light of the sun against a now white overcast sky. The light was unusually bright. It was then that I heard the words: *He can heal.* I stood without moving, but the hair rose on my arms when I heard: *You each possess the means to heal. Align heart and mind. Heal your heart and he will heal.*

I stood staring at the sun for a frozen moment that seemed an eternity, but was in fact was no more than a few seconds. Sensations were pushing into the finer realms of spoken form and found their way not into my brain to exit from my mouth, but beyond it. Many centuries ago, Shakespeare wrote of "Thoughts beyond the reaches of our soul." Passing across my sight came visitors from past and present, unconscious of me and my rapturous stare as they walked across my screen. I felt my heart opening and with it all fear fled. In that moment of awareness I knew I held the power to heal Flash, not in an egotistical way but somehow contained in my desire to forgive and be forgiven.

In that one instant I knew that my mental attitude had far more impact on Flash than I'd ever realized. Living with an open heart and pure motives might just be more important than anything else I could do.

Marcus Aurelius said, "To live your brief life rightly, isn't that enough? Stop talking about what the good man is like, and just be one." I had been given the map to the hidden treasure, and it'd been right here all along.

When I came to, I saw that Flash had teetered off into the parking lot and now sat stuck in one spot. I took a few leaps forward to where he had wobbled and scooped him up. And as I held him in my arms, I turned again to face the sun. It cast its light upon us with dim November rays, persistent and unwavering. I closed my eyes and felt Flash warm and alive against my chest. The voice was gone, but I could still hear it clearly in my mind. Then Marie's words came back to me: "Become the love you seek."

Flash was here in my arms. It wasn't hard to do.

I was tired, but I once more felt the magic of something beginning. The trees along the roadside were turning golden in the lowering light. Does anything matter except being as good as we possibly can, and extending love wherever needed? Maybe true immortality is built on love. I knew my life with Flash was a small thread in the great tangle of life, and like Bogie's "hill of beans" speech at the end of *Casablanca,* our lives didn't matter much in the greater scheme. But somehow I also knew that we were each given these opportunities to learn how to love.

I remembered to look for Route 888 on the way home, and a few miles later there it was. We pulled into the statuary shop and it was with a sense of something greater than hope that I walked up and down through the gray statues—large hounds lying down, angels, Jesus, pigs, and turtles . . . and then all at once, there, greeting me: St. Francis of Assisi.

Inside, a man behind a wooden counter sat puffing on a pipe. He had broken glasses held together with tape. All around, hanging from floor to ceiling, were plastic signs, and knick-knacks and bumper stickers. They were a blur, one becoming the other, but as my eyes focused and I turned to regard the gaudy but whimsical display, my glance landed upon one sign directly across from me.

I felt a current travel up my spine and my skin began to tingle. In large black letters on yellow plastic the sign read *FAITH*. I could almost see Nora standing next to it smiling. But it wasn't this sign that caused my body to react, nor was this the sign I'd take home. I walked over and eased another small sign off its hook from the bead board wall and took it to the counter. While I stood there and the pipe-smoking man blew genie formations of pungent smoke, we spoke of the life of St. Francis. The man told me he had four large hounds at home and when the hour came to feed them they leapt high in the air and it was the happiest moment of his day. Then he was offering me free of charge the yellow sign I held in my hand. It read: *Protected by Dachshund*.

When we returned in the early evening, Chance and Sasha leapt all over us.

"Hi. Hello! I know, I know. It's late," I said to them. "I'm so sorry, but we had an important day." I set Flash on the ground as Sasha scraped her paws across my face and scrambled and squealed with joy.

"I missed you too, Sasha." When I looked up at Chance she was looking back at me. I swear that dog always understood.

Later that night, I spoke with Ted about my decision to try the bloodroot. "Of course, it's not without possible side effects or adverse reactions, but it gives me hope that Flash might live more than two or three weeks." The hard part would be how he felt when I weaned him off the prednisone, which I had to do so the bloodroot could work. Then we'd need to give the bloodroot a chance to begin attacking the tumor, which would initially cause more swelling.

"How long will that take?"

"Two weeks, three . . . ? There's a chance he'll be in greater pain as this begins to happen, but as the tumor shrinks, he should gain his mobility back again . . . and gain time."

Ted was silent for a moment. Then he said, "Do you have two or three weeks to experiment on him?"

I took a deep breath and was about to speak when he continued, "And do you think it's worth making Flash's last two weeks full of pain as he withdraws?"

"They won't be his last two weeks."

Did I believe my own words as I spoke them to Ted? The stress of indecision was back. Was I doing the right thing? Was I deciding to use the bloodroot for Flash or for myself? I wanted so much to do what was right for him, but sometimes it was hard to know. As I went over the pros and cons again and again, and spoke with as many compassionate people as I could, I began to have a sense that, in trying the bloodroot, I was doing the right thing, and with that came strength and renewed hope.

Amy used a pendulum whenever she fell to indecision. She would ask a question and hold the pendulum very still. If it moved in a circle, that meant a "no." A back and forth motion meant a "yes." I called her and asked her if she'd swing it to see if bloodroot was the right road to take.

"Ask it," I hesitated. "Ask it how long Flash has to live. Ask if he'll see the flowers bloom in spring," I finished quickly.

"*If Flash will see spring?*" she said disbelieving. "I *thought* we were going to guardedly shoot for Thanksgiving and be totally amazed and overjoyed if he was here for Christmas. Sorry, but . . ."

"I know, I know, but I just have this feeling that he'll see the flowers bloom." I thought back to that happy moment by the base of our old tree when I planted the bulbs on this birthday and he'd dug with such gusto, kicking up dirt and my bulbs along with it. How could I endure the spring if he had gone from our lives? I knew my wish was impossible based on the vet's diagnosis, but it's what I wanted, more than anything else. Thanksgiving, Christmas, then spring. Beyond spring the picture was fuzzy. I couldn't imagine.

"Okay," Amy answered, but in her voice I heard the concern: her younger sister was losing it. *Honey, swing your pendulum up my chakras, will you, and align me? Honey, I am, like, so manifesting his being here in the springtime. Will you visualize for me?*

I sat and held Flash in my arms. I let my fingers trace the top of his back, which was smooth and felt good where the vets had shaved the rectangle down his spine. I looked at his body, bloated from prednisone. I looked at his useless hind legs and feet, dangling safely in my arms.

"Oh, Flash," I said. "Where do the moments go when we're not in them? How does one passing moment fit into Eternity? Where do our moments with those we love go?"

He looked at me with the face I loved. There was his too-long snout, his one crimped ear, the small, dark eyes. Perhaps he had the answers, perhaps he had not. It all goes by so fast. Each day is its own, never to come back to us again. I looked at my hand touching him and knew that he and I would be ashes and dust in time while the roses would continue to bloom and the trees would put out their green leaves each spring. But for this moment, he was here.

CHAPTER 22

The Decision Made

The longest journey you will ever travel is the journey from your head to your heart.

—ANONYMOUS

I BEGAN TO WEAN FLASH OFF THE STEROIDS.

Amy called in the morning. "I swung the pendulum. Are you ready?" she asked.

"Yes. Go ahead."

"Okay, I swung it twice. Both times I asked, the answer was the same. Are you ready?"

"Yes," I answered again. And these were her words: "Flash will live until spring. He'll see the flowers bloom. But not on bloodroot. You'll find another cure. Not the bloodroot," she said again.

After a pause I asked, "Are you sure you swung it right?" Her snort let me know she didn't appreciate that line of questioning. She replied somewhat curtly that she had swung it, detaching herself as much as possible from the outcome she wanted, and had let the answers come to her. And the answers were the same.

Perhaps I should have listened, but a mind made up is a formidable force, and I'd made up my mind without consulting my heart. I would use the bloodroot to cure to his cancer. How else would he see the spring?

Ted came out to give me support as Flash came off the steroids. I bought Flash a different travel bag, more of a knapsack, and I wore it strapped around my waist so Flash could be with us on walks, and when we were about to go out walking, Ted would say to me, "Bag him up!" meaning, put Flash in the bag.

Ted called it "Flash-in-the-bag" and, eyeing Flash's smug face one day, he said, "He's wondering why he didn't get a tumor long ago," in the deadpan, ironic tone that he had adopted and, but for the twinkle in his eye, I always thought was devoid of levity. And maybe Ted was right. Flash had never been keen on our long walks. How many steps does a dachshund take to each of mine? If it was hot outside, his black body trapped the sun and overheated. And if it was cold, his short smooth coat was not nearly enough to keep him warm and he shivered. He hated the cold. His window for walking was early spring or fall, 65 to 70 degrees, in the warm sun with a slight breeze. When his back trouble began, I left him at home while I took out Chance and Sasha. I missed having him with us but I felt good about doing the best thing for him. I figured he was happier resting indoors than being dragged along on a walk.

One day the girls and I were walking home up our driveway, tired and content, when I heard a strange sound. I might have found it beautiful, had it not held such plaintive longing. It was low and mournful but, like a crescendo, it built in volume at the end . . . and in despair. Flash was not singing, he was howling. Pulling the girls behind me, I ran inside and there he was at the front door, waiting. His lonely lament had stopped but he didn't wag his tail at first. He looked up at me and I understood at once. I dropped to the ground.

"Oh, Flash. We won't leave you again. No, we won't leave you again." Then he was hobbling along after Chance and Sasha and sniffing them all over.

Perhaps love had been behind my choosing the bloodroot. But if so, hope had been my anodyne. Yet it took only two and a half days to I see that I had made a terrible mistake. Day one and day two raised murky doubts. Flash was quickly losing any function he had of his hindquarters, and I was again expressing his bladder. But if those first two days were strained, the third day was unbearable.

Upon waking, I turned over in bed to stare into Flash's now squinty dark eyes. What I saw was a dog pleading for relief. Silent whines escaped his mouth. His abdomen was swollen from holding his back so tensely. Guarded, afraid of the least touch, he tensed his stomach, and it was hard beneath my hand. I reached ever so gently to pick him up, and he cried.

There is a pain so venal, so skilled in purpose, that one might deem it malicious, yet its power lies not in evil but rather evil's opposite, for it is born of love. The pain I felt was my own. As I held Flash in my arms, speaking softly, the enormity of what it means to care for another hit me, and I appealed to a power greater than form. "Please let me take his pain from him. Take from me my well-being, take anything you want, but please give him relief from this."

I knew of the Tibetan practice Tonglen whereby you could take on the suffering of another. I had practiced with Lauren and later with Chance after her snakebite. I stared down at Chance and Sasha both looking back at me and asked aloud, "What should I do for him?" I dropped my awareness into my heart and stood very still.

The answer came in an instant. *Call Rebecca.*

Intuition is that flash of understanding that lies beyond descriptive words. It's the place of unruffled calm that lies in the heart of right action, which no amount of turbulence from outside can touch.

Rebecca Moravec was a friend in Illinois and an exceptional animal communicator. Her niece, Kelsey, was also a friend and a shining example of what is best in humans. Kelsey had long ago suggested I contact her aunt. I'd been calling on Rebecca ever since. Even though she booked up months in advance, Rebecca granted us an appointment that same day. Since I had never cried wolf with her, she knew I needed help. I didn't need someone to tell me Flash was in pain or that he wanted relief, but I did need help in trying to figure out what to do now. I'd been practicing communication with animals for years. I got answers, but were these my own hopes and desires projected onto Flash, like choosing the bloodroot? Right now, I needed to hear from him and I needed a clear and honest answer . . . no matter what it was.

Still, I was not prepared for the words Rebecca spoke. "He is afraid to move because it causes pain," she said quietly. I listened. "He wants relief from it."

"Does he understand what's going on?"

"He knows enough," Rebecca answered. "He needs time. He's in denial. He appreciates your love but doesn't want to talk about anything unpleasant." This rang true, for it was always how Flash had handled life. Where Chance was stoical, Flash and Sasha wanted life to be always easy and fun.

"He has a real fear of not feeling well. And he really doesn't want to be paralyzed. He's afraid and he doesn't want to stay feeling bad," she continued then coughed. Like many energetically sensitive people, her physical body was fragile, more susceptible to others' energies. But she had mastered the art of feeling an animal's pain without taking it on. A lesson I was still trying to learn.

"Can you ask him if he's willing to try the bloodroot? Because it could . . . umm, potentially rid him completely of cancer. The problem is that it, initially that is, puts him through discomfort. He's feeling that now." I waited for her to connect with Flash and form the question. I waited, looking at Flash lying hunched on the bed between Chance and Sasha. Over the years Rebecca had been so uncannily accurate with the ups and downs of the dog life within our home, I could trust her and not question. She had told me about things that were to happen before they occurred, or things about which I was unaware, like the gentle black snake in the basement two days before I found him. What's more, my dogs trusted her and could be honest, for it doesn't matter how good a communicator is if the animal is not willing to tell the truth.

"He just wants it to be completely gone right now," Rebecca said. "He wants to go on with his happy life like before."

I must have let out a cry of sorts, for Rebecca asked if I was okay.

"Let me talk to him again and explain," she offered. I watched Flash as Rebecca spoke silently to him. I watched as one eyebrow twitched, raising up. He was embarrassed. I realized I'd been staring intently at him. I turned my head to look out the window to the yard and the dried grass beyond.

"It stresses him to even think about it," Rebecca said. "He has a terrible fear of being in pain." Yet she was able to do what I would never have thought anyone could do. Flash actually listened and then he spoke of the next phase of his journey.

He said he wanted to feel really good for a while then be done with it if he had to go . . . if he had to leave us.

I was stunned to hear this coming from him, he who disliked even to talk about the times when I had to travel without him, because it upset him so. Rebecca explained to him that I would help him when the time came, and with sorrow I realized it must only have been because he was in such pain that he was willing to consider physical death as a possible solution for relief. I told him that I'd be there with him, always. Then I closed my eyes and opened my heart and asked the question I always asked at the end, "Does he know how much I love him?"

"Yes," Rebecca answered for Flash. "He is grateful to you. He wants to be reincarnated and come back in a healthy body, maybe a bird—a happy bluebird—and fly high in the sky. If he must make a choice, if he cannot stay and be comfortable. He loves you and would want to stay close by. He loves his life. He doesn't want to leave his family. But he's in considerable pain. You see, it is very hard for him to talk right now."

I had held my tears at bay many times over the past month and it was hard, but perhaps no time harder than at that moment. If I cried I knew Rebecca would understand my breach, but I wanted to remain strong for Flash. Chance would understand, although it must have upset her too. And it was Chance who confirmed my decision to stop the idea, and with it the hope, of using the bloodroot.

"She understands," Rebecca said of Chance. "She doesn't want you to worry about her; she's trying to be strong for everyone. She says Flash doesn't want to be in that sick body. She feels for him, but she feels too that death will be only temporary and he'll come back to be with all of you in a strong body.

You have her support; she understands. She worries that Sasha will be a little lost." I stared at Chance and she stood, turned in a circle then lay on her haunches with her front legs extended and began licking her feet.

I told her how much I appreciated her support and asked the same question: "Does she know how much I love her?"

"Chance says she feels your love around her always. She is grateful for your love and she loves you very much. You and she are twin souls." I felt this too. I thanked her again then we moved on to Sasha.

I waited for Rebecca to connect with her. Sasha was lying on her side, and the whole time Rebecca had been speaking with Flash and Chance, she had been preening for my attention, waving a front paw around in the air in hopes that I'd rub her belly.

"Sasha asks that you never put her in the dryer."

I told Rebecca to tell Sasha that I would never put her in the dryer, wondering if perhaps someone had.

"She asks if it will snow again."

"Yes, probably it will snow again."

"She says it's really cold when you put your paw on it."

"Yes, that's right."

"She wonders if you could provide her with a river of cheese."

I laughed, but Sasha was serious and spoke of long lines of bread, cheese, cookies, and cakes.

"She's wondering if you could provide a Fig Newton."

A Fig Newton? I hadn't had one of those in twenty years. "Tell her I think I could provide one."

There was a pause before Rebecca said, "Sasha is worried about your sadness. She doesn't understand it."

"She knows about Flash?"

"She doesn't want to know about Flash. She needs time to process this. She is very much afraid of being left alone."

"*Oh*! Please tell her she'll never be left alone. I'll be here and Chance will be here."

"She thinks Chance has a comforting presence, and she feels your love is a warm blanket. She loves you and her life and is happy. She feels your love has changed her life. But she is reluctant to talk about anything else. Just don't leave her alone."

"Please tell her I will never leave her alone. Tell her I promise I'll always care for her." Then, as Rebecca told her this, I watched Sasha heave a big sigh. I thanked her for coming into my life and asked the last question, "Does she know how much I love her?"

"She does," Rebecca answered. "She loves you back and she is very grateful. She says you're the reason she's so shiny."

I paused. "Because I bathe her and brush her?"

"No. She means shiny on the inside."

I think my eyes got a little shiny then, and I thanked Sasha and told her I would always keep her shiny. I was about to conclude when Rebecca said that Chance had something more to say. I waited. Chance seemed to have been biding her time to say what she really needed to tell me. When Rebecca spoke, I was unprepared for Chance's words.

"She is telling me to tell you that you must do what Flash wants. You must do right by Flash."

Tears stung my eyes. I said I promised to do right by Flash and thanked her.

When I got off the phone, I was a different person from the one who had, with renewed hope, dialed seeking an immediate answer. I had received my answer, not from Rebecca but through Rebecca. I had received my answer from Flash and from Chance. But it was not the answer I'd wanted. So often they never are. I realized, as I would realize again and again, that my only job was to trust.

I had to do right by Flash. My great "knowing" about the bloodroot was dashed. My trip to North Carolina and $265 a waste. But not really, because Flash and I experienced that road trip together. Together we bought the St. Francis, who would watch over us in the days and months and years ahead. Yet when I first put the statue in the yard, all three dogs had barked at it. Sasha darted into corners of the yard, hackles up, terrified. It took days for her to get used to the statue's solid presence, and I realized her fears were based on illusion, just as perhaps mine were to some greater being looking down upon us. If courage was simply the act of hiding your fears, I was going to try it. I wondered if Sasha would sign up too.

I retrieved both the steroids and painkillers from the cabinet where I had shoved them away, and slipped Flash one of each. Once the steroids took effect, I would stop using the painkillers, but right now my only desire was to alleviate his suffering.

There we sat. Chance had known. I must honor Flash's feelings. A new decision had been made. We were going to use the steroids, if only a minimal amount, and opt for quality of life, rather than the bloodroot and a possible cure for his cancer. Perhaps my heart had known all along. Still, I cannot pretend that this was an easy decision for me to make on many levels.

Yet, in many ways it was the easier decision for, I see now—with the hindsight whose intelligence is painfully obvious—that this was the higher decision. Death may be birth's opposite, but it's not the opposite of life. Only a small part. Death would just mean trading in his dachshund body for a new one—his soul forever connected to me, to Chance, to Sasha, and to Lauren.

I knelt and held him in my arms before the woodstove and together we watched the flames dance and leap. The fragility of his body made me realize the impermanence of life and in that moment my love expanded. It was the love I always felt for what was lost, for already I had glimpsed my life without him, the days ahead where memory would become my strongest ally moving me through pain and tears until finally, it rested in joy. But through this knowing and recognition of the inevitable I had a stronger sense that everything worked out the way it was meant to . . . that I would never really lose him. I felt the soft pressure of his back foot against my arm. I closed my eyes and let my fingers run over his legs, his paws, the smooth pads underneath. I could feel his body relaxing as the medication began to work. I wanted him to be with me always, but even more than that, I wanted him to be free of pain.

Outside I could hear the urgent wails of a siren growing closer and closer, a sound that had scared me as a child. As the ambulance passed our house, Flash threw his head back, singing for all he was worth with the sound of the siren. Chance and Sasha raised their heads, then rushed over to join him. "*Oooooh, aroooowwww, rep, rep, rep. Yow, wow, wow!*" Then as the sound of the siren faded, one dog would stop and another would begin; it was the sound of odd instruments—a tuba, an oboe—warming up before the symphony. And I sat on my haunches with Flash in my arms amidst a cacophony of horrible, wonderful noise.

When the siren had passed and the serenade came to its end, we went outside. Earlier the air had felt full of rain; now it just felt fresh and pure. I often asked myself if, after death, I were to be given one day back on earth, what would I do? You would not find me before my computer screen, however much I love to write. No, you would instead find me sitting on the ground, surrounded by the dogs, feeling the grass beneath me. I would tell them I loved them and feel their love for me. Then I would simply sit and be. And this was what I did.

It was November 15. We had used up two of our three weeks. Although fall had come everything seemed to deny it. The air was soft and warm. When I looked up at the viburnum above us, I imagined the spring blossoms amongst the dark red autumnal leaves, confusing memory with nostalgia. And at that moment I realized for much of my life I had traveled to exotic countries seeking to enrich my small life. But now I saw that I had found joy in my own backyard.

"Thank you for teaching me to slow down," I said to Flash. My column could wait. So could the lecture on Burgundy. What I needed was to be outside with my dogs. "Thank you for showing me how to live in the moment the way you do every day." He was heavy in my arms, and I pulled him closer to my chest in a gesture I remembered from childhood with stuffed animals. I would protect him forever. Chance and Sasha sauntered over to where we were sitting. The dried brown grass beneath us was healing. Sasha sat down and stared at me, then nudged my arm for her turn in the lap of love. Chance yawned then stretched. And Flash sniffed the air.

A peace enveloped us, pushing through my sorrow. When I stopped trying so hard to be mindful, I found that I was. Perhaps it's true that there really is no time. As I sat on the grass with my dogs, I felt only love and gratitude, and not the passing of time. And in that moment with them beside me, there was nothing more for me to want.

As the drugs took effect, Flash hopped off my lap. He sat contently staring down the yard at something. Then he was digging and biting up grass roots the way he loved to do. I sat for a long time watching him. The light changed. I wanted the memory to stay with me, but experience told me that it too, like everything, would fade, becoming one with the shades until all merged, blending and connecting, with no beginning or end.

Proust said, "We don't receive wisdom; we must discover it for ourselves after a journey that no one can take for us or spare us." I looked to Flash and thought of his journey. I thought of my own, and the two journeys that bound us together. I began to see that it was not any career or title or accomplishment I had achieved that made me who I was but rather these pure moments of awareness together with the dogs and the natural world. They made up the most essential part of my life. And perhaps in this way, together, we touched Eternity.

CHAPTER 23

Susie

If you bring forth what is within you, / what you bring forth will save you. / If you do not bring forth what is within you, / what you do not bring forth will destroy you.
—Jesus, from *The Gnostic Gospels*

We're connected in life by a web so essential but fine we often fail to see it. In 1971, screenwriter Ted Perry, inspired by the wisdom of Chief Seattle, wrote: "This we know. The earth does not belong to man: man belongs to the earth. This we know. All things are connected like the blood that unites one family. All things are connected. Whatever befalls the earth befalls the sons of earth. Man did not weave the web of life, he is merely a strand in it. Whatever he does to the web he does to himself."

In the kindergarten class my mother taught, she would ask the children to choose a life form to pretend to be. It could be the sun, the air, water, a blade of grass, a farm animal—just about anything you could think of, even humans. Then she would ask the child pretending to be a horse for instance, what he needed in order to live. The horse would reply, "Air." And she would run a string from this child to the child who was air. "What else do you need, horse?"

"Well, water. And sun and grass." This would form three more threads in the web.

This went on until the class was one big crisscross of string, the web of life. The lesson was that everything needs everything else; we're all connected. John Muir said it this way: "When we tug on a single thing in nature, we find it attached to everything else." While stretching the strings from one child to the next and stepping over them, my mother had to be careful not to break the web.

The web of life I kept stumbling across was one over which I thought I had no control. Yet the more I stumbled, the more I realized it was actually made up of chance encounters and coincidences, all organic and interconnected with one another. The momentous events in our lives may seem to stand alone, but are in fact made of many small decisions along the way.

I had spent so much energy searching for a cure for Flash that I didn't at first realize it was when I stopped trying so hard that the cure showed up. It came to me as a vague recollection of a kind woman named Susie in the parking lot after one of my wine tastings. But why was I recalling her now? She had told me she worked with copied energy signatures, a kind of complex homeopathy or total body analysis (TBA), and the example she gave me was that of a young boy with cancer. She explained that after taking the drops the boy had recovered.

I rummaged through my papers, hoping I'd saved her card.

Three hours later, Flash and I were driving the back roads to Susie's for our first visit. She had offered to see Flash whenever I needed, free of charge. The least I could do was pay her for a session for myself.

Flash lay sleeping in the front seat beside me. Outside the landscape changed from the gentle mountains surrounding our home to large tracts of land and real working farms. Silos and cattle. The sun was out and I lowered the window to let in the pungent air. Then the farms gave way to miles of strip malls, Walmart, Home Depot, Lowe's, McDonald's, Sheetz, outlet stores. Following her instructions I turned onto Ladd Road and drove past modest brick ranch houses. I had the sense that all of these families led happy, uncomplicated lives. Leaves had fallen and the countryside was painted with soft strokes of brown, gray and white. I could make out the shape of now leaf-less sugar maples in front yards, those same trees which just a few weeks ago had been a burst of color. The forsythia had been pruned back and would not bloom again till spring. Patches of snow traced the edges of shadier lawns. A plume of smoke rose from one house and I thought with longing back to my own home and the woodstove. I looked at Flash and, sensing my glance, he opened his eyes. Finally I turned into Susie's sub-division, sparsely dotted with expensive homes and beautiful, manicured lawns.

Most people put on a public mask when meeting new people or talking to strangers, but when Susie answered the door to Flash and me, I felt her warmth at once and knew that I could be myself with her. She had reddish brown hair, blue eyes, and an easy smile, but the spark which lit her from within was her authenticity.

The house was large, clean and quiet. She led us up a stairway to her work room. There Flash and I sat down for what would be the first of many visits.

"Do you want me to tell you what's going on?" I asked, holding Flash on my lap.

"No, you don't have to."

She pulled out sliding trays of many different liquid vials and told me that she would use a form of kinesiology and test each one against Flash. She did this by tracing her fingers across the array of vials and muscle testing with the opposite hand. She explained that the TBA practitioner has more than one thousand samples of various antidotes and, through a precise protocol, the practitioner is able to find the primary systems that are out of balance, then track those to a series of antidotes that represent every probable cause. This includes viruses, bacteria, parasites, genetics, previous traumas, and much more. There were vials for all the major organs within the body as well as skin and bones, eyes and teeth . . . literally a vial for everything. If, for example, a dog had tapeworm, Susie would get a "yes" when she muscle tested against that vial. I found it was best to try to accept her practices without the need for analytical explication. Perhaps this is why Susie had been successful treating animals—they had no preconceived notions about the process.

All I had told Susie was that Flash had been diagnosed with cancer. She knew neither what kind nor where. She knew nothing about his limited prognosis.

I sat back in the chair and stared out her window to an apple tree, to the vast front lawn and houses in the distance. It felt good to have Flash there with me. I felt hope rise in a new kind of way.

"Do you get a tumor?" I asked her.

"Yes."

"Malignant?"

"It is." She said looking up to me. "I'm picking up his spinal cord."

"That's where it is."

"But I'm also picking up on lungs. Does he have trouble breathing?"

My heart sank. I tried to take a deep breath myself, and didn't answer for a space of time. Flash was nodding off in my arms. I let my fingers massage his funny feet. Then I explained that the doctors had said the cancer would most likely metastasize to his lungs.

"We'll do what we can," Susie said, sensing my shift in energy. When she was finished testing through the drawers of tubes with Flash, she had a fistful of glass vials.

"Is that a lot?" I asked her.

"The most I've ever seen." She looked at me sadly but kindly. A healthy person or dog would show maybe eight or ten vials. Susie tested everything from the cellular level to the metabolic level, possible diseases, vitamin deficiencies, and viruses. She also tested for one's emotional and spiritual well-being.

"Did anything show up for Flash?" I asked when she was going through the emotional states.

"Yes," she answered, giving me the name of a particular Bach flower essence. "It means he tries to put on a cheerful face even though he's suffering."

I swallowed back the pain of her words, which were in many ways harder to hear than the physical diagnosis of cancer. "*Oh, Flash,*" I whispered down to him. I pulled him into my chest and kissed the top of his little head. There in my arms, at least in this moment, he seemed at peace with his lot.

Susie fastened a rubber band around all his vials and placed them on a machine that copied their signatures. When the light on the machine turned off, she handed me one small, brown glass bottle with a dropper.

When she finished with Flash, she tested me. I ended up with my share of vials too, which surprised me, as I had always felt healthy. Susie said the primary concern was my heart: coronary arteries, pulmonary valve, bicuspid (mitral valve), interatrial septum, right atrium, and on it went. I wondered if maybe she'd made some mistake. This bit of information was not what I needed at that particular moment in time.

Susie saw my apprehension.

"It's not unusual to have a lot of vials on the first visit. Just take the drops," she said gently. "You can come back when you need to. I won't charge you for Flash."

She explained how to take the drops. For me, half a dropper three times a day, five minutes away from food. I mustn't let the dropper touch anything. For Flash, the same thing: I would simply raise his lips and squirt the liquid onto his gums. Before leaving I gave him his first dose and he accepted the drops quietly, the way he'd accepted all of his treatments. I made a mental note to bring Chance and Sasha to see Susie as well.

As we left the subdivision and drove back past the ranch houses, I felt Flash relax beside me. I looked to the lowering sun neither realizing how well I would come to know these roads nor the significance they would play in our lives. As we rested at a stoplight, I saw the orange sun begin its descent behind Home Depot, and I saw that beside me, curled up, Flash was sleeping peacefully. Whatever the future held, I had this quiet moment.

CHAPTER 24

Heart Medicine

Love is a sacred reserve of energy; it is like the blood of spiritual evolution.

—PIERRE TEILHARD DE CHARDIN

IF I HAD NEEDED TO VERIFY SUSIE'S ANALYSIS, I RECEIVED my answer three days later from my allopathic doctor when I went in for my yearly physical, although in my case "yearly" was somewhat of a misnomer. It had been more than four years since I'd had a checkup.

As I sat flipping through a magazine, surrounded by geriatrics coughing, I questioned my sanity on whatever day I'd had the great idea to schedule an appointment. Where was the harm in one more year?

I'd begun taking my drops but in truth had forgotten about my heart, so focused had I been on Flash, so that when my doctor listened to my heart and frowned, I should have been concerned. And when a nurse hooked me up to the EKG machine, I was so tired I fell asleep with the cold, sticky suction cups attached like tentacles to my breasts, feet, and stomach.

"You can get dressed now," the nurse said undoing the sucky things. "The doctor will be in shortly."

Again I sat. Again I waited, flipping through the pages of my *New Yorker,* and for several minutes I was gratefully lost in its fine reporting. Sometimes mundane moments, like those in which you return to a place you've been to in the past, had the power to distract from preoccupation with the problem. For a few minutes my mind was freed from Flash. But no sooner had I realized this with a sense of relief did I at once feel the simultaneous guilt.

When the doctor knocked, I came back to the room with difficulty. He sat down to share with me the odd news that my heart was not functioning as it should.

"What does it mean?" I asked.

He cleared his throat and took on an avuncular expression to show his concern. "Have you been under stress?" he asked in his low voice.

"I have," I said and smiled, feeling the old familiar need to put those around me at ease. Or perhaps on this day I felt there was nothing left to do but laugh in the face of life.

"Have you considered, ah . . . talking with someone?"

"You mean you want me to see a shrink?"

"It can, in many cases, prove helpful."

"I'll think about it," I said to appease him. "My dog is . . ." But I couldn't finish. "I don't think therapy is the answer to my problems . . . however much I wish it were," I finished.

"Have you tried methods of relaxation? In our busy, stressful world, this is very important."

"I meditate. I walk my dogs. Do a little yoga."

"Get adequate sleep?"

"Try to."

"How's your diet?"

"Vegetarian. Can't blame red meats." I tried to joke again.

"You're healthy in many ways. But stress can . . ."

"Stress can kill. I know."

"I'd like to recheck you in a month or so."

I took a deep breath. "Okay."

I don't know why I didn't worry over my own heart's diagnosis. Perhaps that's just one of the many blessings Flash gave me. There was no space for it next to caring for him.

In retrospect it's easy for me to see—though perhaps less easy for a conventional doctor to understand—that my heart was truly broken. There weren't words to express what throbbed within that place behind my ribs. Only feelings . . . and they lived and breathed inside my heart.

CHAPTER 25

Welcome to the World of Miracles

Our true home is in the present moment. To live in the present moment is a miracle. The miracle is not to walk on water. The miracle is to walk on the green earth in the present moment, to appreciate the peace and the beauty that are available now.

—THICH NHAT HANH

AND THEN THE PEACE.

The peace came slowly but, like a relationship that is built upon friendship and respect and not merely wild attraction, I sensed it was here to stick around. It happened one night shortly after our trip to Susie and the doctor.

I sat up in bed surrounded by my three dogs. Outside, the silken light of a half-moon transformed our strip of yard into a ribbon of light. I stared at each of the dogs, my eyes finally resting on Flash and in that moment, where I might have felt the choke of panic or the drain of depression, there was peace. Gently, from nowhere, the peace befell me nudging out the stress, and I felt profound serenity in the moment.

I laughed as if a joke had just floated by. Then silence again, as the soft orange glow from the salt candle blanketed the room in tranquility and warmth. Beside me, Flash breathed deeply. Chance was curled next to him, offering him, her quiet strength. And Sasha stretched her plump body around him as if protecting him from further harm. In my state of grace I slipped into a moment so beautiful I was scared to move lest it leave. I stayed very still . . . and it persisted. And again the silence . . . except the light sleeping breath of the dogs.

I said to myself, "I accept where we are and what's more, I trust." We would not use the bloodroot and this was okay. We would trust in whatever future we were given and that too was okay. I think the acceptance of the situation together with an open heart brought us to a place of infinite love, and in time and with a distanced perspective, I would find it easy to accept Flash's fate, even my fate with the restaurant, and see how all the pieces fit together. Cliché as it sounds, true growth rarely transpires in gentler times so we learn to welcome the pain. Because waiting on the other side of pain is peace.

By morning I knew I was different.

The way I understood reality was changing and this could apply to Flash or to anything else. I began to see miracles as the norm, not the exception. When I relinquished the need to control the outcome with the bloodroot or with my lover and surrendered instead to letting life live through me, the universe stepped in and the miracles began.

I looked over at Flash just as he shook, his ears flapping against his body and making that sound I loved. It was the sound of well-being. I lifted him off the bed and he shuffled along, his back hunched up, walking over to his dog bed but not without first taking a bite of dirt from one of the potted plants. He scrubbed his face and head against the dog bed with the delight of being alive in a rallying body, then gazed out the window, watching for field mice and birds.

Time, as we measured it, stopped making sense. Moments like these warped time, one moment stretching it, another moment shrinking it. As the rest of the world seemed to speed up, following advances in technology, we were slowing down. I found I no longer cared what other people said or thought of me. What does it really matter what anyone thinks except ourselves and the Divine? Marcus Aurelius said it this way: "It never ceases to amaze me: we love ourselves more than other people, but care more about their opinions than our own. . . . Don't waste the rest of your time here worrying about other people—unless it affects the common good. It will keep you from doing anything useful."

Another shift that occurred was that I began to love all beings. I began to see that except for a set of conditions over which I had no control I might have ended up with Flash's littermate and not him . . . or any other dachshund who needed rescuing. Where had Flash's littermates gone? What is the fate of all the abandoned dogs in shelters, or worse, laboratories? What would Flash's fate have been had he not come to me? Had I ended up with Flash's sibling would I not have loved that dog with the devotion (and inevitable emotional attachment) with which I now loved Flash? And I would never have known Flash. If perhaps I were to see Flash on the street at the end of a long leash held by someone else, I might have walked over, knelt, and stroked him once, but I would not have felt the same attachment. Yet Flash would still be Flash. And I would still be me. And it is unimaginable for me now to think about any twist of fate in which he did not come into my care. Would this other person at the end of his leash have paid for his surgeries? Would he have eaten good food and had a nice backyard, or would he have suffered at their hands, chained outside on a dirt log? I cannot imagine my life without him in it, just as it is inconceivable to think of who I might have become without Lauren, Chance, or Sasha.

I began to realize that because of these dogs for whom I cared, loving them must mean loving not only all dogs, but all animals, and all beings. If I had intellectualized this long before, I had not lived it completely. But once the shift occurred I could not go back to being the person I once was.

Perhaps it was this feeling that opened wide the door to my heart and began healing Flash. I will never know. But I did know that as the unconditional love began to pervade my thinking, each day casting out more and more of the old useless thoughts, I found the greatest reward of all—quiet joy throughout my hours.

Even if I could not see this gentle joy, I knew it extended out like an aura, its energy permeating my house and those around me, including Flash. I knew that having a loving heart was more important to his healing than I could express. No veterinarian would prescribe it, but neither could they disprove it. It was these feelings, however mysterious, by which my soul began to live. Because of Flash's diagnosis, the resolve to become my best self grew in leaps measured now by joy and serenity and from that was my compassion for all life fostered.

That evening I spoke on the phone with Dr. Sid Strozum, one of the more alternative vets in the area. I kept him updated on what treatments I was trying with Flash. When he explained to me what would have happened to Flash had I opted to use the bloodroot, I felt goose bumps up and down my arms.

"I can certainly understand why you would be tempted," he said, "but the most likely outcome would be initial swelling and inflammation. The problem is that, enclosed within the spinal cord, the swelling has no place to go . . . to expand. The out-come would not have been good, no matter how you look at it. It would involve not only tremendous pain but also paralysis."

I listened and when he was done, I thanked him. I hung up, and stood still a moment allowing his words to sink in. When I turned, I saw three pairs of eyes watching me.

"Come on," I said. "We're going to the river."

I felt Flash against me in his bag as we walked beneath the bare trees in the eerie glow of early evening. Golden light reflected in the puddles across our grass trail. I kept hearing Dr. Strozum's words in my head. When we reached the river, Chance and Sasha did not ford as they normally did but remained on the banks, their heads down, scenting. I stepped out into the moving water in my rubber gardener's shoes with Flash and squatted to touch the cold water.

I always felt that if I could just hold on to a moment like this and remember how it felt, it would be with me forever, a constant by which the rest of life's experiences could all be measured. I know now that these moments, while a part of us always, are inherently unattainable if willed to come forth. Truth and wisdom are not gifts you gain then retain forever, but something you practice, something you work hard remembering and living, day in and day out.

And what strange paradox that we are never more alive than when we stand face-to-face with death? I stood in the river a moment longer, my pant legs getting wet. There was beauty and peace, but also passion—the passion for life.

When we returned, I lifted Flash from the bag and set him down on the grassy trail. I turned my back and walked ahead with the girls. When I turned around, Flash was not sitting on the ground in the same spot, but following along slowly, carefully. It was the most he had walked since his surgery. I dropped to the ground and as he came closer and closer my vision grew blurry. When he reached me, I scooped him up into my arms and together we sat looking up to the autumn sky. Then I put him back into his bag and we walked home through the dimming light.

CHAPTER 26

Living the Shift

We are not human beings having a spiritual experience.
We are spiritual beings having a human experience.
—PIERRE TEILHARD DE CHARDIN

THE FIRST DAY I REALLY KNEW SOMETHING HAD SHIFTED WAS a day I called "the day of the deer." I rose before dawn and walked outside into the new morning air in the phantom hour, before bird or beast stirred. I stood quietly listening to the sound of the infinite. Without the silence, there could be no sound, just as without the pain we don't fully know joy. I had learned not to push away suffering but, crazy as it seems, to welcome it, for I think it's only through our own pain that we become more deeply aware of the suffering of others.

Just as the sun was cresting the mountain tops, I slipped back inside to lift Flash off the bed and nudge the girls, who jumped down. As we watched the dawn break, I stepped up onto the old apple crate table, holding Flash. He surveyed the fields beyond, sniffing the cool new air from a tall person's vantage point. All his life he had wanted to be bigger. This was one way he could . . . at least for a few moments in time. We stood gazing out to the mountains beyond, and I had the recurring thought that it was such a small corner of the world, such a tiny piece of all that was. But as I felt Flash warm against me, I knew it was enough.

After the first truths of illness, there is often a moment that descends upon you unbidden like a gentle nursemaid hired to alleviate the stress of days to come. I stood in the first light of dawn with the dogs, letting the morning breeze wash us clean. But for the shaved strip of hair upon his back, Flash would have looked as healthy as any other dog. Diamond glints of sunlight sparkled through the trees.

I ran back inside to get the leashes and Flash's bag. He was walking more but still could not cover long distances. The dog pack solved this problem. I wore it strapped in front of me and nestled Flash in. My shoulders suffered the brunt of his weight, but if they argued the point, my heart won out.

On the day of the deer, I strapped his bag around my waist, hoisting him in and folding a soft Tibetan blanket Amy had given me over his back to warm him. I kept the girls on long extension leashes, only letting them off to hunt for rabbits when we approached small, observable thickets.

As we walked across the hushed morning fields of dried grass, the breeze touched my face and the feeling of joy that had greeted us upon waking stayed with me. It was not unlike the feeling of being in love except without the delirious physical component. It was more akin to feeling in love with all creation. I was surrounded by so much beauty I felt I had the power to right all the world's wrongs. I knew love was the means by which suffering and abuse ended. I loved the very men who tortured animals, even if I didn't love what they did, for I realized on the soul level they were no different from me. I realized that until we loved the people who did harm, those whom the world deemed unlovable, the suffering would continue.

We walked up into the hills behind our house to where two creeks converged and made a waterfall. In the confluence of the mountain streams I stood and felt the life of the woods building behind the hushed morning silence. In the stillness of the trees, there was wisdom.

It was then that the deer appeared. Two does leapt from nowhere and landed a few feet from where I stood with the dogs. They must have been as startled as we were to find amidst their water supply this foreign little group. But the feelings of love were still with me and without thinking I tried radiating love their way. What happened next astonished me.

The two deer stepped closer. One stretched out her nose to sniff at Flash. Then the other was stepping toward me. She was so close I could have reached out a hand and touched her velvet nose. I saw the girls' stance change and their tails straightened behind them. I stared at the doe for a protracted moment before Chance and Sasha, at first as stunned as I was, lunged forward on their leashes, and the deer leapt away. Flash twisted in the bag and yipped in excitement. I touched his head. "I know. I know." He stopped and I stood for moments more listening to the sounds of the deer grow fainter until there was again the silence of the forest around us.

"Come on. Let's go," I called and pulled gently at Chance and Sasha, who were still posturing, sniffing the air and staring after the deer.

With Flash snug in the bag, and Chance and Sasha trotting out front in scent-heaven, we were high on life. I decided we would walk up farther in the forbidden fields. The forbidden fields were those which bordered the one I called the magical field, but lay closer to where Mr. Jake lived. The part of me that felt so good was tempting fate, and with it came the childlike thrill of doing something prohibited.

I looked over the treetops to the light clouds, aware that there was so much I would never understand, and I wondered why Mr. Jake had to make life harder for us all. The fields skirted his driveway and we had to walk up it a little way to reach the magical field.

I had the feeling you get when emboldened by alcohol. I felt invincible. Perhaps the feeling had to do with the deer or perhaps with Flash being alive and well. As I walked I was aware of the footsteps of the past, not only my own and Lauren's, but of those, human and animal, who had treaded the same earth before us. There was the sense of being part of something larger, and in that way the insignificance of our lives melded into the multitude of lives preceding us, and created one beautiful whole.

The magical field was protected by low rolling hills rising up on every side. It lay there undetected like an exquisite china bowl someone had hidden and forgotten. Partway down something else caught my eye. At the edge of the field stood a scraggy tree I knew well, but it was still laden with brownish orange fruit. Shriveled, post-frost persimmons.

I began to run and as I did, I was a child once more.

The fruit looked rotten, and I thought of the oyster. What brave soul had eaten the first? Many persimmons had already fallen to the earth. We stood by the side of the meadow in the hush of the trees, and I could sense the animals that ate from this tree. I plucked one shriveled brown ball no bigger than a small plum. As I brought it toward my nose and sniffed I could detect no smell, and when I broke into the skin it was not only with a sense of foraging, but also with a sense of the forbidden.

Flash raised his nose to my hands and I said, "Wait just a minute." The gelatin flesh was pumpkin-colored and there were dark brown seeds like a watermelon's seeds. We often saw them scattered amongst the bear scat on the trails we walked.

I knelt and slipped Flash from his bag. Then I pulled apart the small, brown persimmon, making sure to peel away the bitter skin. I tasted the first bite with closed eyes. *Butterscotch.* It was like the candy I remembered on Halloween. The dogs sat before me waiting. Chance broke into a pant. Three noses sniffed the air, but eyes remained fastened on me.

"Okay, ready? Try this." I handed out bits of the orange flesh, careful not to give them seeds, which could cause stomach upset and impaction. They loved the persimmon fruit as I did. I was about to pluck another, when all three dogs began to bark like crazy and a strong yet unfamiliar scent reached my nose at the same time. Its pungent spice was like nothing I'd ever smelled before and as I inhaled, I knew someone was behind me. There was a drumbeat in my chest and, despite the cold, sweat began under my arms and at the sides of my neck. My attention focused on the fruit, I'd lost track of all around me. These thoughts and sensations cut through my mind in a split second, and I was still semi-crouched, holding the fruit in my fingers when I heard the voice behind my back.

I turned around to behold Mr. Jake. The dogs were wild, barking with hackles raised. I thought we could cut into the woods and run, bushwhacking our way home. But it was Flash, loose, who took up the challenge of protecting his girls from the intruder.

Rep, rep, rep, rep! With his tail crimped and back hunched, he charged directly toward Mr. Jake.

"Flash, no!" I yelled. Still clutching Chance's and Sasha's leashes, I scooped Flash into my arms. But he squirmed loose and was back on task, barking and leaping up against the man's leg, and I saw Mr. Jake swing his foot back in a motion that could only mean he intended to kick Flash.

I remember going to the fairground with Amy long ago and agreeing to ride the roller coaster even though it scared me, and as it carried us up and down against my control, I'd felt how powerless I was to stop life's events.

"*Flash!*" I leapt forward, but Mr. Jake's foot hit Flash solidly, and Flash faltered and fell. But then he was up, and staggering back toward Mr. Jake. I lunged for him but Sasha had wound her leash around me and I stumbled.

Rep, rep, rep, rep!

"Get away from me, you stinking rodent!"

Mr. Jake kicked again at Flash again but missed, and I leapt, hurdling my leash-entwined legs toward Flash. This time I got him and held on, and for a moment, I was oblivious to Mr. Jake and the wild world into which we tumbled. Still tangled in leashes I ran my hands over Flash's body. By the struggle he put up to get to Mr. Jake and continue their game, I assumed he was not only unharmed, but in full attack mode.

Then I heard the words: "If I see you again, I'll kill him." It was as if the words came from nowhere. Only then did I look up.

The trail was not level, and even though we stood on higher ground Mr. Jake towered over us. He was huge. He wore a gray overcoat that billowed out in the breeze, terrifying Sasha, who was barking relentlessly, her hackles raised in terror.

"Get your dogs off this land and don't come back," he said. But it was what he next said that sent a chill through my body.

Looking directly at me, he spoke in a tone devoid of reactive emotion: "That dog is going to die."

I untangled the leashes and backed up holding Flash while pulling Chance and Sasha. There was nothing I could say. I glanced to his waist quickly looking for handguns. I felt safe in the knowledge that he wouldn't kill us if we were actively walking away from his fields. I kept trying to form a response: apology, defense, explanation? But no words came. I turned my back to him and walked methodically back down the drive. I was unaware of the sun on my face, or the clouds in the sky, or the trees lining our walk. Unaware of anything except the girls trotting by my side, trying to turn back and bark, and me jerking them forward to keep walking. And Flash in my arms still, not even the bag, my hands running over his body, feeling his bones and muscles for breaks or tears.

When we reached the end of the drive and stepped off onto our land, I dropped to the ground. My heart was beating, *Thump a thump, thump.* I felt all the contained emotion erupting as the autumn sun shone down on us. Flash peered up at me, looking energized from his encounter with Mr. Jake. I let my finger trace the vertebrae along his back. I took a deep breath. One conscious breath. Then another. "Oh, Flash," I said to him. "You are so brave but . . ." He stared into my eyes, eager, as though he expected praise. "Never mind. You are so very brave. So very fine." He pricked his ears, listening. Then, as I breathed in and out, all I felt was relief.

Back in the house, I checked Flash over again. I put him on the floor and made him walk forward. He didn't limp. By a miracle he truly did seem fine. He flopped into the dog bed where I covered him with a soft blanket. Then I replayed what had happened. Why did Mr. Jake say what he did? He'd said Flash would die. I shivered, feeling superstitious. Did he know what he was saying? And wasn't it against the law to kill someone's dog? Even an evil trespasser's dog? How could he say we couldn't walk over his land? Those walks were our life. I would write him a letter. No, I would call him and arrange for a one-on-one meeting. Maybe ask Nora to come too, in case he killed me. But no, I didn't want her killed as well. I would meet with him in a public place. The questions sped through my mind, in the way they do that leaves no room for observation. I felt the need for silence but try as I might to quiet my mind, it continued to race.

I stepped outside again and knelt before Lauren and asked for guidance. The air was still—the kind of stillness you need to hear clearly. Out of this stillness I heard: *You're not upset for the reasons you think. It's not about Mr. Jake and the land. You must be the person you want to be at all times. Not just the easy times. And you can. Who are your heroes?*

"Flash," I answered back.

Apart from him.

"St. Francis of Assisi," I answered. "And Mother Teresa."

I listened to the silence around me.

"And Gandhi and Marcus Aurelius and Albert Schweitzer and . . . Jane Austen."

Then make them proud. Be the person you want to be.

I knew this voice was coming from within me, not without. It was my own voice, yet it felt like the voice of wisdom, that part of me that was always kind, wise, and compassionate. That part that knew and saw all.

I heard the dog-door flap behind me and turned to see Chance walking out. Then Flash, then Sasha. They walked over to me as I knelt on the ground. Sasha shoved her nose into my hand to be petted and Flash laid his head against my thigh.

"You okay?" They pushed into me and I reached out to include Chance. "You all are such good dogs. I mean *great* dogs. Really great dogs."

I brought Flash into my arms and stood. Thought slipped from my brain, and as I rested without my mind's noise, the feelings and sensations grew. There was the smell of dry leaves, evoking holidays past, those that stamp their essence in childhood, the yardsticks by which, for better or for worse, all subsequent holidays would be measured. There was the overcast sky and I could recall the football games we played, stumbling and fumbling on the wide lawn of cousins in Philadelphia. Just standing and staring at silhouetted trees against the now setting sun I could summon the sensation of lying on my back, cozy in bed, and waking to the smells and sounds of my mother in the kitchen. The sweet smell of butter mixed with brown sugar, or pancakes sizzling in a large cast-iron frying pan. The light outside changing as it gave way to morning.

That night in bed, I read for a long time, then turned to look at the three dogs sleeping. Chance was jerking beside me, chasing rabbits in her sleep. Sasha breathed deeply, contentedly, now that she was safe from the bad man. Soon she would begin to snore. And Flash was out. His nose lay twisted to the side and I saw it twitch a few times, but apart from that and his slow heaving sides, going up and down, he didn't move. I thought about Mr. Jake. "Even to him, I'm going to send nothing but love."

I replayed the incident again. Then I remembered something he said. I turned to Flash. "A rodent! Flash, he called you a rodent. Is that why you attacked?" But Flash was not going to dignify that question. With eyes peacefully shut, he was replaying his own version of the day's wild events.

CHAPTER 27

Miracle of Love

When we come upon beautiful things . . . they act like small tears in the surface of the world that pull us through to some vaster space.

—ELAINE SCARRY

ON NOVEMBER 2, FLASH WAS DIAGNOSED WITH CANCER AND given three weeks to live. On November 23, the three-week mark, I stood at dusk and looked down at him sitting beside me in the grass. He sat in his characteristic slung-back position, slightly turned so that one hind leg poked out from under his steroid-swollen body. His head was raised and I saw his nose twitch a few times as he sniffed the evening air—air deeply steeped deep in the scents he loved.

"I love you," I whispered. They were the three words I had so often said to him, and to Chance and Sasha.

For a moment he remained sniffing the damp air. I kept my eyes on his face, until he turned and looked at me as if to say, "I know, I know. I love you too. Don't embarrass me."

I scooped him into my arms and climbed up onto the crate table. I saw him casting his glance around from the safety of my arms. Below us Chance and Sasha watched, also smelling the cool air. When Sasha saw movement and barked, Flash emitted a little yip.

I thought of our lives together. Thirteen years. What I had wanted had been so simple and yet perhaps a little selfish. To have him with me still. But I could transmute the selfishness, for in loving one, I found my love extending out, encompassing many, and maybe it's always through the individual that we touch the universal. Standing there, with my dogs around me, I was surrounded by a rich yet soundless peace, and I knew its provenance was love.

Maybe the very least we can do is live quiet, yet purposeful lives, and not worry about saving the world through heroic acts. Because, at the end of the day, it's not the heroic acts that make up our lives and matter most—there are too few of them for most people—but the small acts of working and living and loving. For this reason I didn't get caught up in politics or the world's great dramas, because I saw time passing through them. Yet the little acts mattered . . . and in this way, became big. Flash's illness and limited prognosis created a sacred space, characterized not so much by urgency as by serenity, and it was here in this sacred place that I wanted to stay.

CHAPTER 28

Thanksgiving

Vision is the art of seeing things invisible.
                                        —JONATHAN SWIFT

IT WAS NOVEMBER 26. I WALKED UP THE STEPS TO MY FATHER'S house on Thanksgiving Day. In my arms was Flash. The sun was low in the sky casting shadows, but I felt the last of its warmth touch us like a blessing. I paused for a moment as I thought back to that day in room 217 when the young vet explained Flash's diagnosis; how I had seen Thanksgiving and a future that passed barren and joyless without Flash. Now I cradled his body against me as Chance and Sasha sniffed their way up the front walk. When my father opened the door, there was the exaggerated fanfare over Flash, the remarks people make when they realize the importance of some event but don't know how to dress it with adequate words. The same way that, as we hugged one another, we made all the insignificant yet indispensable greetings we humans need to cross worlds and connect.

I let the girls run around the elegant house and settled Flash onto the sofa beside me. There in the living room my father, his wife Margaret, Amy, Ted, and I gathered in front of the fire as the soft light of late autumn enveloped us through the large windows. I opened a bottle of François Chidaine Vouvray, a

160

delicious golden Chenin Blanc that a few talented producers in the Loire valley have perfected to an art form.

"Here's to envisioning the impossible."

"To miracles," Amy said, raising a glass.

"To believing, knowing, and not giving up," my father added.

As we toasted each other and life, the birds hopped from branch to branch outside the windows. The sun slipped from behind a gray cloud, illuminating its edges, and for a moment we were all bathed in light. Flash asked to get off the couch and I set him on the ground where he padded down the hall to investigate the house for mice. Chance snatched a piece of baguette off the coffee table when she thought nobody was looking and Sasha gave me the long-suffering look that said she was hungry and I never fed her.

At the table, Flash sat with us, a shiny, black vision, gently reminding us all of the art of imagining what seems impossible.

"Maybe nothing is impossible if you want it with all your heart," I said with newfound confidence.

"Then no parent would ever have to watch a child die before his or her eyes," Margaret said gently.

"Well, there's a point. Then . . . why do we have to go through such pain as humans?"

"How about opening the Burgundy first," Ted said, staring at the bottle of Chambolle Musigny like he might pop the cork through the power of concentration.

"We know what you're grateful for this day," my father said to me as he pulled the cork.

I smiled, reaching over to pet Flash, who my father and stepmother were kind enough to let sit at the table with us. Yes, I was grateful . . . more than grateful . . . but where were words to express what *was*?

"I'm grateful for aged Burgundy," Ted said, raising his glass and winking at me. "And for Flash." Then without missing a beat, he continued, "Why do we go through the pain? So we'll enjoy moments like these all the more."

"But murder, war . . ."

"The point . . . ?"

"Just that humans can be so incredibly horrid . . ."

"And so incredibly beautiful."

"The duality of life."

I thought of all the millions of people in the world and how we brush up against one another trying so hard to connect. "And sometimes we find that touch of love in the oddest places," I said aloud. Then as the wine and food flowed, we talked and laughed, and I ate vegetables and bread and reached for pieces of turkey, "accidentally" dropping them to Chance and Sasha, who waited patiently under the table while Flash dined by my side.

How was it that one small dog could teach me so much about life? I was learning not only to cease worrying but also to surrender and trust.

In the ebbing afternoon that followed our Thanksgiving meal, I drove home and built a fire in the Writing Room. Flash was outside in the yard rooting around for rodents. He wasn't having much luck. But my luck was different. I'd received an email from an agent expressing interest in a story I'd written about Flash.

I called to him and the girls, and watched as he walked the length of the yard that once he could not. Then he was walking up the long ramp that covered the four steep steps to the Writing Room. I clapped my hands. "Come on, Flash!" It was such a small thing, but to me it was everything.

I lifted him onto the Writing Room sofa and Chance and Sasha jumped up next to him. Then all three were digging and circling making just the right nests. I smiled at their various efforts and looked out the window to the world beyond them, to the remaining leaves of the sycamore tree swaying in a passing breeze. Puffy balls still hung from the tree, silhouetted against the sky, incongruent and beautiful. The dogs began to doze, and I thought how easily and unexpectedly we can find beauty and joy.

Like a breeze that ripples over a lake bringing whitecaps to its surface, the air moved through the few remaining leaves and, as it did, they fluttered and spoke. For every step of this journey I was relying upon my heart. In fact, my heart was my only guide. I can say that I was never once led astray when listening to my heart, while my mind had taken me down ragged, broken roads.

I had stopped writing in my journal about the sensations I felt were beyond words. If I "forgot" on a literal level, I was assured I'd remember, without the need for written prompt or recall, those moments which, shared, feared, or celebrated, were formed from love. These were what I'd remember, impressions that will, I hope, stay vivid with me . . . until I too fade away, finally following those I love.

CHAPTER 29

Love Is the Answer

One word frees us of all the weight and pain of life. That word is love.

—SOPHOCLES

THE NEXT DAY, I WALKED INTO THE SHOP AND SET FLASH down in the office.

"That you, sweetie?" I heard Marie call from the kitchen. She'd been home in Joyzee the past week for Thanksgiving. "Jesus, Mary, and Joseph, you won't believe what Louise said to Robert and Gracie."

I had my head down reading messages when I heard her come in behind me. I waited for her to catch me up on all the drama of nine siblings convening in one household for Thanksgiving dinner, and ensuing brotherly and sisterly dysfunction that was as much a part of such gatherings as the second piece of pumpkin pie and whipped cream.

I looked up and took her in fully for the first time. "I'm sorry, I got preoccupied. Let me give you a hug."

"Jesus, Mary, and Joseph," she said stepping back from me, "What have you done?"

"What?" I asked. "Do I have food on my face?"

"Your aura. You're glowing. Look at you."

164

I stared back.

"You're . . . like a different person."

"How?" I asked quietly, hanging on to each of her words and watching her face take on an odd expression. Flash was lying peacefully in his bag by my feet.

She began to speak, but I interrupted her. "Look, Marie, he's *here*. They gave him three weeks to live, over three weeks ago. He's right *here*." We both looked at him, lying with his head over the soft mesh of the bag.

"You're living in the miracle zone. That's what it is. Sit, sit, we need to *tawk*," she said with a bit of urgency. And she wedged herself onto the edge of the filing cabinet. "Now you need to help your dear friend Marie. I love my family but I've been trying to take care of them for close to fifty years and all I get is more of the same and ten extra pounds each decade. If this keeps up I'll have all the reality shows calling me, and . . ."

"You're a giver," I said, interrupting this healthy train of thought. "Givers want to fix everyone. But you're seeing that you can't fix them. You can love them but you can't fix them. Givers give so much that they ultimately end up giving all of themselves. Start giving to yourself, beautiful one."

Marie stared back at me. "I'm supposed to be saying all that to you."

"So it's my turn now." I smiled. "Tip the balance back. Send love. Love them. That's the only thing."

"What'd you do?"

"What do you mean?"

"I can feel your aura, and what's more I can *see* it."

"Yeah?" I was intrigued but more than a little skeptical. "What's it look like?"

165

"It's purple and lavender and blue and it's got this golden, silvered light all around," she said, staring not at me, but at my . . . edges.

"You're making that up."

"Making it up? Don't forget who you're tawking to. What I want to know is—Jesus, Mary, and Joseph—what'd you do? Forgive me, but you were one big walking mess when I left for Joyzee."

"Oh, Marie . . ." I wanted to tell her everything, but I didn't have any idea how. All I managed was, "I think it's been happening slowly all along, but I think Flash was behind it."

"And?"

"And . . . I listened to my heart?"

"Do you think that's really it?"

"Marie! That's what you preach!"

"I know, but I've tried so many different things . . . hypnosis, positive thinking . . . and none of it seems to work."

"They're all good, but I doubt any one thing holds the answer . . . you know?"

"Do I ever! I picked up a free booklet the other day and was leafing through it. I was reading all the ads for the classes and treatments: Hatha Yoga, Tai Chi, Qigong, Zen meditation, essential oils, flower essences, fasting, Polarity Therapy, Zero Balancing, acupuncture." She paused but then the fountain of New Age youth continued: "New Birthing, Tarot, Crystal Therapy . . . then I realized, I'd tried them all."

I laughed but she wasn't making a joke.

"My God, what haven't I tried? . . . this diet and that diet . . . What's left? Ayahuasca and psychedelic drugs and . . ."

"Good red wine and a really good book?"

This time she laughed when I wasn't trying to joke. But then we both were laughing, and I felt the wisdom in our laughter in a way that perhaps all the spiritual advice in self-help books could never give. "Maybe we just need to slow down."

"And *love*," she said, sounding more like herself.

"Yes." And maybe the answer was much simpler than we could imagine. Maybe we just needed to be here and to be present every single moment and . . . love what *is*.

Marie began to ask the obvious question and I answered her aloud, "Which is what Flash showed me."

"You've turned something terrible into something beautiful."

"But it wasn't terrible. It was heartbreaking, yes. But ultimately beautiful . . . for both of us, I think. Marie, people will tell you, you need to make money or get some corporate job."

"Or win the lottery."

"That you should be doing all these important things and that sitting and doing nothing is not good. But all you need is to put aside the mobile devices for one moment. Step outside. Sit down with your kids or your dogs or your friends. Love matters. Sit down in silence. And then listen."

Marie cocked her head and put her hand to her ear. "I don't hear anything."

I reached over and put my hand on her heart. "Hear that? Listen . . ." I saw her begin to speak then stop. I saw the tears forming and I saw her pushing them back.

"What you've done is the greatest miracle of all," she said.

"I didn't do anything."

"This is no time for secrets." She put her hand once more to her ear theatrically. "Is that reality TV I hear calling?"

"I guess I just opened my heart and let it come through me. Flash was the conduit and . . . when they told me he was going to die, I realized how much I'd always loved him, but maybe taken his existence . . . and this beautiful life we're all given . . . for granted, and I . . ." I was searching for the words to explain to her, when I saw Marie had shoved her knuckles against her mouth and was crying. I put my arms around her and I felt all the anguish for her family that she'd been holding or repressing, but also . . . all the love.

CHAPTER **30**

Visualizing Christmas

We must be willing to get rid of the life we've planned, so as to have the life that is waiting for us.
—JOSEPH CAMPBELL

WHAT STOPS US FROM HAVING WHAT WE DESIRE? I HAD BEGUN to align my head and heart and think more with my heart. I had begun to imagine "the impossible." I began seeing Flash with me on my birthday, December 17.

While part of me was almost afraid to hope for this, another part of me simply knew. It was a different feeling from wanting something very badly. When we're in desperate need of something, we can block the desired result from happening. But when we relax into knowing, what we desire comes naturally. Rumi said, "Observe the wonders as they occur around you. Don't claim them. Feel the artistry moving through and be silent."

When I had the knowing, I felt empowered and strong, and in those moments I'd make sure to spend time visualizing positive outcomes so the worry and doubt of weaker moments would not overtake me.

It seemed an impossible wish, but I wanted to have him not only alive and well on my birthday, but also feeling well over that magical holiday season I have, since childhood, always loved. The visualization I chose was very specific and concrete. I saw him at my mother's where we always spent Christmas morning, digging in the carpet amongst the scattered bits of wrapping paper. I told Amy and my mother to hold this image too.

"Speak only to the wise," said Goethe. I knew not to share my hope with too many people, however, as most people, in trying to be "realistic" and not wanting to see me hurt when my dream failed to pass, would try to steer me away from the impossible and try to prepare me instead for the inevitable. Vets and other well-meaning people pointed me in another direction, warning me that the chance of Flash living to Christmas was a million to one, and I should be preparing for a life that would not hold Flash in the long days and nights ahead. But I had stepped away from that outcome, taking Flash with me, and I think he was as grateful as I was.

Amy was visiting me one day when an idea came to me.

"I've got it," I said.

"I've lost it too. Years ago."

"I said I've *got* it. I know what I'm going to do. I'm going to buy three ornaments, one for each of the dogs. I'll wrap them now and open them on Christmas Eve and hang them on Lauren."

"The tree."

I could feel a loony-little-sister comment about to burst forth from her lips, and I raised my hand as if to ward it off. "Don't say it."

"Don't have to." She smiled, and I could see she was actually intrigued with my ornament idea.

We set out trying to find the right ornaments, wooden dachshunds, crystal stars, something of that sort. 'Twas the season, and commercialism and obscene gaudiness were in the air. There were inflatable Santas and snowmen, flashing Rudolph the red-nosed reindeers, and the ever popular penguins that inhabited every discount store. We searched but nothing was right. Until we walked into a local crafts store and found hand-painted ornaments made from ostrich eggs. Each was painted in its own geometric, pagan, or Middle Eastern pattern.

"They're perfect. Elegant and natural," I said running my finger over the surface of one.

"I don't know," Amy said, eyeing the ornaments askance as though the mother ostrich was in the next room just waiting for the wicked person who would buy shells made of her firstborn.

"It doesn't mean the baby ostriches were killed," I said and selected a large one in pale pinks and greens for Flash. "These are only pieces of the shells. The baby ostriches have hatched." Then I selected two smaller ones in oranges, yellows, pinks, and greens for Chance and Sasha.

"If I were you, I'd ask the ostrich gods for forgiveness tonight just to be sure," Amy cautioned.

"Okay. I promise."

I felt pleased, but the strongest moment of knowing came later that week as I put the ornaments into their boxes and got out the wrapping paper. As I wrapped each one individually, writing the dog's name on the outside of the package, there came a moment of doubt, piercing and powerful, but as quickly, the fear was replaced by trust. I had to trust that I really would be unwrapping each small box and hanging each ornament on the tiny tree . . . with Flash still alive. I had to feel it with every cell in my body.

That same evening I pulled out a sketch pad and some pencils. I drew a picture of myself kneeling before the pine tree in my backyard. I drew Flash in my arms. I drew Chance and Sasha looking at us. I drew a shining moon. And I drew a bright star above, sparkling through the darkness. Beneath the sketch, I wrote the title, *Speaking in Miracles*.

That night before I climbed into bed I asked that "compassion encircle the earth for all beings everywhere." Then I added a special request for all of the ostriches around the world, that they might live pain-free, full and happy lives. Somewhere, I felt Amy smiling along with many ostriches.

Soon thereafter I developed another visualization. Perhaps to keep from dwelling too heavily upon Christmas I began to see Flash hopping in and amongst the spring flowers. I began to see him rooting around in the yard. I saw him walking through the blooming bulbs I had planted on his birthday in October. To those people who lived with miracles, I could say with great conviction, "Flash is going to see the spring." And I'd ask that they picture him beside the spring flowers.

"Yeah, pushing up the daisies from the wrong side," a sarcastic friend teased.

"I don't think so," I said without offense; I was feeling too much joy.

Judy Carman, the author of *Peace to All Beings: Veggie Soup for the Chicken's Soul*, responded to me right away. "Kay, I know that Flash will see the flowers bloom." Judy's words became our mantra. *Flash will see the flowers bloom.*

Gandhi said there is more to life than increasing its speed. Flash, Chance, Sasha, and I were all slowing down. This did not mean that we were dying. In fact we were doing more, and I felt reborn. Well, actually we were doing less and being more.

172

I was realizing that by doing less I could achieve more: more love, more joy, more being, more feeling, more of real life. When I sat out in the yard with the dogs—not reading or gardening, but doing nothing—enlightenment landed lightly on me like springtime moths and butterflies. In these moments of stillness, brief moments of presence when I stepped outside my head, the miracles came. I began to ask myself hard questions and, when I came out of these enlightened states, I found the answers to my questions always waiting.

Was there a time when I had taken Flash for granted and worried instead about some trivial problem? And if this was true with Flash, could it not also have been true with others? Then how could I blame them? I couldn't.

The problems in our lives lie not within the actions of others or external circumstances, they reside within our own hearts. Is it such a radical idea to think that the world could change overnight if each of us looked deep within our hearts, addressing the negative while cultivating the virtues? Were we to do this instead of directing our attention to what was wrong in others and the world around us, we might find our own greed and envy dissipate, and when greed and envy aren't motivating factors, we no longer abuse the earth or her creatures for our own gain. I had only to close my eyes and feel the incommunicable rumbling of my own heart . . . and with that, forgiveness for all, and . . . love for all.

CHAPTER 31

Winter

To forget time, to forgive life, to be at peace.
—OSCAR WILDE

AMY ALWAYS TOLD ME THE PATH OF WISDOM IS PAVED WITH silence. As Flash began to recover from his terminal diagnosis, I remained silent despite my desire to shout it out to the world. There are things about which one talks, and things about which it is appropriate to remain silent.

At home I kneeled before Lauren or the statue of St. Francis and spoke to the universe through them. "Please help the dogs behind shelter fences, the domestic animals crammed into small cages for human consumption, and all the laboratory animals behind bars so far removed from their natural sun and light." And with my prayers, I would send them my love. Sometimes I recalled, and was comforted by, a few lines from the Talmud in which it instructs: "Do not be daunted by the enormity of the world's grief. Do justly now. Love mercy, now. Walk humbly, now. You are not obligated to complete the work, but neither are you free to abandon it."

To most people my instincts told me to be humble about Flash's miracle, otherwise it would become something else.

I was driving him back and forth to Susie's but I knew many people would be skeptical about this too, so again I kept silent.

That winter we were blanketed with more snow than Virginia had seen in fifty years. A storm before Christmas stopped traffic for days and filled our yard with twenty-two inches of heavy, damp snow. When the snow hardened on top like the coating of a crème brûlée, the dogs could walk on its surface. But the surface was slick and Flash's already unstable feet splayed out, as his toenails tried to grip onto ice. I began the task of digging trails for him and the backyard became a maze. Birds hopped and pecked at seeds and Flash weaved his way in and out of huge mounds of snow.

The dogs went out less and less. They stayed inside huddled together in one dog bed or followed the warmth of the sun as it settled into different corners of the room. There I'd find them all vying for the same bed in the sunniest spot. Once, Flash was hidden under a blanket when Sasha trotted over to the bed and lay down on top of him. I jumped up to nudge her, but Flash didn't seem to mind, his head and nose poking forth from Sasha's bottom, so I let them be. All three loved the woodstove, and the bed in front of it was their favorite spot. I'd walk in to behold one furry clump of dogs, Flash invariably in the center using the girls' body heat to warm his own sparsely covered frame.

Then came the second and third storms, blowing in from the northwest and dumping down a fine powder upon our already wintered world. Winds uprooted trees and tore down utility wires, and where towering piles of snow had been turning gray from soot, now the world was again washed white . . . at least for a while.

At the shop customers walked through the door and the first thing out of their mouths was about the weather.

"Do you think it could snow a little more?"

"What happened to mild Virginia winters?"

"I didn't move here from New York to get stuck in this."

"People down here don't know how to drive."

"It's awful. It's just awful," the lady standing at the counter awaiting her cappuccino agreed.

"What is awful?" her young daughter asked.

"The *snow*," her mother answered.

I turned my attention to the espresso machine and not the white world beyond the windowpane which was providing a reserve of water for trees in spring. I thought of Flash—he was here. Spring would follow winter. It always had. I served the cappuccino, then stood staring out the window to that frozen world. Minutes passed before I realized I was being addressed.

"*Miss?*"

"Oh, I'm sorry," I answered. "More coffee?"

Yet the weather could also serve as something that bonded people together. We were all experiencing it. Mother Nature assumed no favorites.

"Hear more snow's coming. Just finally got my car dug out," said a man at the front table sipping a cup of strong black coffee I'd just brewed.

His friend, an older, white-haired facsimile, grunted.

"And if the weathermen can't get it right . . ." He stopped and turned to the door as it opened and a young woman rushed forward, letting in the cold, damp outside air.

"Sally Rose." I nearly knocked over the coffee as I ran to hug her. "How are you?"

"*Oh, Kay,*" she said, in the sweet tone she always used. "You have *no idea.*"

"What?"

"Remember what I told you about my boyfriend?"

"Yeah."

"After I talked with you, I went back to him thinking I'd tell him we had to break up," she blurted to me and the old men sitting at the front table. I steered her away from the hungry ears, watching the dimples in each of her cheeks deepen then disappear then deepen again. "But before I had a chance he told me he left her. He left the girl he's been trying to leave . . . he left her for *me.* He said he was committed to *me.*" She was beaming and crying and trying to talk all at once. And I loved how she kept saying the word "me."

"*Oh, Kay,*" she said again with light shining in her eyes. "There's so much love in the world."

"Yes," I smiled.

"If you open your heart to it. Everyone just wants to be understood. To be *seen.*"

"Yes."

"I think somehow your words that day . . ."

"*I* didn't have anything to do with it," I said, laughing with her.

"You called me later, remember? And you spoke to me about being the light, but also about welcoming the darkness because in it are stars. Stars, stars, stars! I love the stars."

"I said that?"

"And you said that someday I would look back on that terrible, difficult time and feel its beauty and understand why it happened, and that I would be able to look back from a place of joy and new courage at how far I'd come. You said the sorrow would all make sense one day."

I stood listening to her, not remembering having said it, but feeling her words touch the place I found myself standing.

"Oh, Kay. You have no idea . . ." She didn't finish. She only smiled and asked, "Where's Flash?"

I led her around to the other side of the counter, away from the drafts of cold air. There Flash dozed in his bag, his nose twisted to the side as it tucked under his thin, whip tail.

"Flash! Like that little bit of tail is going to keep you warm!" She shrieked and I felt her delight in seeing my malformed little dachshund. When she bent down to kiss him, I thought she was going to try to get into the bag with him and warm him up.

The door opened again, letting in the smell of pine and winter. In walked Jane, one of our many faithful customers.

"Kay! Sally Rose!" Jane exclaimed as she hugged us both. Everyone knew everyone else. You could leave your wallet at home and tell the shopkeepers you'd come back the next day to pay. You could leave your car and your house unlocked. One woman bought a cake from us, and when we didn't have a box to put it in, we simply said, "Just bring the plate back tomorrow." She was astounded and because of that one gesture, she decided to buy a house and move to the area. These were only some of the many reasons I loved living in the little town, which not only had no stoplight, but also no stop sign, and I hoped it'd stay that way for a long while.

I saw tears had formed in Jane's eyes.

"How're you doing?" I asked, knowing that her husband David had just moved on to the next phase of his journey after a long battle with cancer.

"I have to tell you this one story about David just before he died," she said. And though I had places to go, things to do,

I relaxed as I listened to her. I realized my work was as much about listening than it was about anything else.

"I was sitting with him and he was pretty out of it, but all of a sudden he just looked at me, looked me directly in the eye, and said, 'Is that a new sweater?' 'No David,' I said. 'I've had this forever.' 'Well, I've never noticed the angel right there before,' he said. And he pointed right to my chest." Jane was crying and we squeezed her in a big hug sandwich.

Later that day I looked out to the magical winter world and I thought of Jane's story and of all the things that were beyond my empirical knowledge, but things I somehow understood nonetheless without having to understand why or how. It was hard to believe there would come a time when flowers poked through the earth's cold-coated skin, but beneath the snow, I saw the beauty of spring, held deep within winter.

CHAPTER 32

Healing Continues

The mind creates the abyss, the heart crosses it.
—SRI NISARGADATTA

THE FOLLOWING WEEK WAS MY RETURN TRIP TO THE conventional doctor. Again the depressing waiting room where most of the people were afraid to smile. No one even made eye contact. The fluttering of magazine pages. A man's cough, furtive.

I found myself getting frustrated that I'd wasted this day for outside the sun was shining and, although the air was cold, I could be home walking my dogs. Then I remembered that these sorts of thoughts would not help my heart and in fact may have gotten it into this trouble in the first place. I realized there was nothing I could do about the wait. I was here and I'd chosen to come. Nothing to do but accept it and change my attitude to one of graciousness. Flash was not only alive but doing well. Christmas was nearly upon us. I silently blessed the gray-haired lady beside me. Did she feel it? At that very moment she glanced up at me, and I smiled. Behind the sagging skin I saw her blue eyes twinkle and for that moment I saw her as a twenty-five-year-old with her hair blowing beside some beau in the back of a convertible. She'd been young once. I'd be her age one day.

Then I was being summoned by the nurse and I forgot the old woman who had morphed for a moment under my gaze.

The nurse hooked me up to the EKG machine, but this time I didn't fall asleep. And when the doctor sat across from me in the examination room and explained that my heart was 100 percent back to normal, I was only mildly surprised.

"It's rare to see a comeback this fast or this complete," he said. "Might I inquire what you did?"

But all I could do was laugh. When he didn't respond I mumbled that I'd gotten enough sleep. "I always eat well. I tried to get a bit more exercise with the dogs. They appreciated it." But I couldn't tell him about Susie's drops. He had been trained conventionally. And I couldn't tell him that I'd spoken with my heart every night telling it how much I loved it, after I told the dogs how much I loved them.

Perhaps all my aching heart really needed was to fall in love again with life and all it offered. I realized once more how little we know of the mystery of life, how it can hide behind sorrow and pain and still offer light. How it lives in the smallest of things: the flower's smiling face or a ladybug as she makes her way from plant to plant—the simplest things, scattered along life's path. And most days we walk right by. On this day, I simply thanked the doctor for the good news and walked back outside to my car, to the snow and the cold, bright light of December. I was going home to be outdoors and walk my dogs.

CHAPTER 33

Christmas

Love is . . . like a spring coming up out of the ground of our own depths. "I am a gift." All that I am is something that's given, and given freely. Being doesn't cost anything. There's no price tag, no strings attached.

—THOMAS MERTON

BACK WHEN FLASH HAD BEEN GIVEN HIS THREE WEEK-sentence, would any of my family have dared to believe that he would be with me on Christmas day? Probably not. Because, in loving me, no one wanted to raise false hopes. And yet *I* had been the person who dared to believe, and each night as I lay down beside the dogs, I knew that I could not give up.

On Christmas Eve, after dinner with my family and Flash, I drove home to Chance and Sasha and walked outside onto the snow-covered earth. I knelt before Lauren, and in my hands I held the three Christmas boxes containing each dog's ostrich ornament. I unwrapped each one slowly, saving Flash's for last. Then I hung them on the tree. I called to the dogs and only then, with Flash in my arms just like the picture I'd sketched, did I let myself cry the sweetest tears of all.

On Christmas morning, we gathered first at my mother's around a six-sided game table before convening in the dining room. Flash, Chance, and Sasha sniffed around the house, but hung out mostly in the kitchen awaiting the odd treat or piece of fallen food. Tippy, my mother's dog, was in a corner wondering why the house had suddenly been invaded by aliens, although it was Tippy, the result of a German shepherd impregnating a Jack Russell, who looked more like the alien. Amy's two big salukis, Dream and Tasy, gave our gathering elegance. And my sister's other two dogs, Coe, a pit/Lab cross, and Ziggy, a Min-Pin (who more accurately resembled a fruit bat), added still more color and confusion. My mother was in the kitchen putting the finishing touches on the traditional Christmas brunch. Cooking was her passion and she loved putting together the seasonal meals we all remembered from childhood.

"There are no sticky buns this year," she called to us.

"What?" Amy shrieked as if someone had just told us the baby Jesus was an imposter all these years.

"None of us needs all that butter and sugar," my mother said from the kitchen.

"But it's tradition," Amy protested, as if sticky buns were the whole point of Christmas.

"Some traditions are meant to be broken," Ted said, refilling his glass, much happier that champagne had trumped the sticky buns.

"Croissants and popovers?" Amy asked.

"Of course," my mother said walking in. "And scrambled eggs, holiday bread, toast and marmalade, potato cakes, bacon . . . and soy sausage," she said looking at me. "We're not throwing out the baby with the bathwater."

"Interesting how traditions evolve," Waverly, my mother's partner, said. "Things that work well one year are repeated the next year and the next and become traditions. Traditions give life a continuity that creates a feeling of security."

"And give us stability and structure," Ted added. "Even illusory stability and structure."

"Sticky buns give structure," Amy said, but forgot that line of reasoning when my mother plopped the basket of freshly baked croissants on the table.

"Continuity creates a feeling of security," I repeated, watching Flash. He sat on the carpet surrounded by the discarded wrapping paper, and I took his picture.

"Illusory security," Ted said softly. "But that's something."

The sun popped through the quilt of clouds and we sat for a moment thinking our private thoughts. Waverly turned on the stereo to play carols in the background and, when "It Came upon a Midnight Clear" began, we were suddenly all singing along with it as best as we could. When the song and our own rendition ended I asked Flash, "D'you want to *sing*?" And without a moment's hesitation he threw his head back in a most exuberant manner and started *ooohhhh*ing and *awwroooo*ing, the whites of his eyes showing as he peered around, perhaps in great singing zeal or perhaps impressed with his attentive audience. Tippy barked and Dream joined in, singing in a beautiful low bass, then Chance, then Sasha, then Tasy. When it was over, I said as I always did, "Thank you, Flash. Thank you all for that beautiful song. I don't know which song it was, but it was a beautiful song."

"It was 'O Holy Night,'" my sister said, as if I was the biggest imbecile ever to sit down upon Christmas morning. "Couldn't you hear the high notes?"

My mother angled the crystal sphere hanging in the window so that the light reflected and scattered over the walls and floor. She told us the dancing light always reminded her of her mother, our Grammy Kay—my namesake—who had died many years before. She said that behind the pain and grief of death, love was what survived.

"*Get it,* Flash," I said. And Flash pounced, chasing the flashes of light.

It was only much later in the day that Ted, with his eyes on Flash, said to me, "You know he might not be here next year."

"I know," I answered. I knew that Flash could not live indefinitely. I stared at him there amongst the presents and colored paper. "But he's here now." And I had a feeling that I would remember this Christmas for a very long time.

CHAPTER 34

The Miracles Expanding

There are many things in life that will catch your eye, but only a few will catch your heart. Pursue those.
—MICHAEL NOLAN

I WALKED INTO THE SHOP WITH FLASH SLUNG OVER MY shoulder to where the usual stack of bills and requests greeted me. "How on earth and I going to deal with these?"

"Maybe you could call Oprah."

I glanced up to find Marie standing in the doorway. Her attempt at problem solving was often interesting. But, at that moment, Oprah seemed more viable than any plan I'd managed to put forth.

It was only after several hours that she came back into the office.

"Forgot to tell you something. The building inspector was by." I looked up, a sick feeling in my stomach. "He said we're fine. We're free to go on."

There was a pause while her words floated around in my brain, arranging themselves and taking shape. "*What?*" I asked. But she only smiled at me. "Are you serious? Why didn't you tell me first thing?"

"It was never that important to me. At least not enough to *worry* over. Anyhow, we're good. We'll go on serving hot soup and making people happy as long as we want." She beamed and I could only beam back in return.

~~~

That night I called to the girls to go out one more time before bed. I thought about the building inspector and how easily Marie had pronounced to me his approval. And I thought—not for the first time—that life works itself out in the end. Just then Chance trotted out, stretched, sniffed the earth a few times, and squatted. Sasha stared at me from an armchair like I'd asked her to fold the laundry, and then ran and jumped up on the bed, settling herself in for the night. I lifted Flash from his dog bed, walked outside into the night air, and set him on the ground. He too sniffed, then found Chance's spot and, proudly raised a leg, marking it as his own.

I stood beneath the stars, looking up. The stars were sparkling pinpoints across the black sky. Chance brushed by me, popping in through the doggie-door to join Sasha in the bed. I looked for Flash down the yard, dark against dark. I couldn't see him, but I knew he was down there somewhere, probably poking his nose through the fence at whatever scents lingered on the other side.

In the January sky, Orion hunted tirelessly, his belt pointing to Sirius, the dog star, in the south and to Jupiter in the north. I couldn't see the dog star. But perhaps like a faithful hound at a master's side, Sirius was helping Orion, hunting just below the mountain range where my eyes could not travel. But there, always, just the same.

CHAPTER 35

Flash Sees the Flowers Bloom

If the sight of the blue skies fills you with joy, if a blade of grass springing up in the fields has power to move you, if the simple things in nature have a message you understand, rejoice, for your soul is alive.

—ELEANORA DUSE

TWO DAYS AFTER MARIE GAVE ME THE GOOD NEWS, TED WAS at my house and he called me to come outside. I was in the kitchen making lunch, but I stopped. There was something in his voice. My mind jumped to Flash and I walked out to where Ted was standing in the front yard. My eyes traveled to the spot where he pointed and there, popping forth from the earth I saw one, then two, yellow crocuses.

"Get Flash," Ted said, and I ran back to the house without a word. When I walked back out through the front door, I let Chance and Sasha loose and carried Flash in my arms down to the front yard and the first yellow blossoms. I watched as Ted jogged to retrieve his Canon from the car and I watched as he strolled back, grinning at me. Then I placed Flash beside the blooming flowers and Ted took his picture.

For a moment no one spoke, and I felt as if we were in some strange and beautiful trance.

"He did it," my brother said to me breaking the spell and lowering the camera. We both stood staring at Flash beside the flowers. Ted was shaking his head back and forth as people do in disbelief. "I didn't think he would."

My chest ached then, the same way it had when Flash dug up the rug on Christmas morning. Scientists say that the vagus nerve goes into spasm when we look upon an image that moves us deeply. Our chests expand, sometimes we tear up, and it's impossible to speak in the space of those moments. I didn't speak and Ted stood beside me, and Flash sat next to his flowers.

I still have that photo. Of Flash beside the first yellow flowers.

Two weeks later was March 20, the first day of spring.

A few hyacinths pushed their cheerful faces through the earth, and the daffodils rallied close behind. And at night I could see the yellow forsythia sear into the darkening sky. The air around us had softened. It spoke in whispers but I understood. Soon everything would burst with life.

I wrote in the morning, but as quickly as I could, I leashed up the dogs and together we set out down the road. We walked up to an abandoned house where there hung a wooden swing. I tied Chance and Sasha near a pile of wood, letting them sniff for past occupants, and lifted Flash onto my lap. I settled into the swing and began to pump my legs the way I once had as a child. Flash sat with equanimity in my arms and we sailed high, trying to reach the treetops, then swooshed backward toward earth. Perhaps he felt the same freedom that I did and that delicious bottom-dropping-out sensation, or perhaps he loved reaching heights his small stature had never before allowed as we flew high up in the tree branches like the birds he tried to catch. The sun warmed our faces and I watched his nose twitching, sniffing. Flash was flying. I saw his ears lying back against his head in an expression of contentment. Then they lifted lightly as we sailed downward in flight through time and space, and I knew then that ordinary life, with all its messiness and pain, but also all its glory, was enough. Finally, thinking of the girls, I stopped and set Flash on the ground to let him try his legs for a while. I guess no one can stay in sublime heights forever.

I stood and felt the warmth of the day on my arms and face, and smelled the rich, fertile scents that oozed from branch and leaf and signaled the start of spring. Then with Chance and Sasha on leashes and Flash trotting along, we continued. All at once I knew where we were going. We were going to the magical field. If Mr. Jake shot us, we'd die happy.

Up the hill we climbed together. But after a while I stopped and scooped Flash into his bag. I was just lifting Flash when Chance let out the noise Ted said sounded like a baby walrus being kicked. Springtime meant baby bunnies. I knew the rabbits were faster and more nimble than the beagles, so I unclipped the girls' leashes and watched them hunt, secure in the knowledge that they wouldn't catch a bunny, but also understanding that hunting was what they were bred to do and, in this way, they could (and should) do what they most loved. Around and around in circles they went, storing scents in their snouts I'd never smell. Chance's legs stomped up and down while Sasha sashayed her body from side to side. Both feathered their tails back and forth wildly. Flash watched the commotion but didn't try to struggle from his bag. Light spilled through a gap in the clouds and the birds called back and forth to each other.

"Okay, come!" I shouted after a while. They didn't come and would never come to me when on the scent, so I snuck up behind each of them. With tongues a-loll and bodies shimmering in satisfaction, they beamed up at us. I clipped leashes back on and we continued. Underfoot I felt old leaves mixing in with the new grass. I stepped carefully over uneven ground, over sticks and rocks, and Flash's head and nose bobbed to my step.

It's odd, but the body often knows something before the mind. And the dogs knew before I did. They didn't bark or bristle, but something in the air had changed. The sense of smell is the most primitive of the senses, one which humans tend to overlook, but to a dog, it's the whole world. Perhaps, without consciously realizing it, I had picked up from them the knowledge I would later call sixth sense or inner guidance. Over the years they'd taught me to think with my senses, not just with my brain.

I started walking slower and slower. I remember looking to one side then another watching for deer or quail, or for the coyotes that howled to us at night.

We crossed Mr. Jake's drive and walked into the magical field. There was an alertness to our movements as if some part of us knew to watch out. A light breeze moved through the branches, raising new leaves upward. A big black crow chased after a hawk. My eyes were skyward for a moment until Sasha's low growl brought my focus back to earth.

I saw the dog before I saw the man. Standing in a corner of the field as if guarding something. He must have smelled us at the same time we saw him, for he turned his head and I saw his hackles rise. I stopped, still unafraid at that point, though cautious. I recognized him as one of the hound mixes that ran loose from the neighbors. With probably some shepherd blood mixed in with hound, he made an imposing sight.

I didn't dare set Flash on the ground; he'd charge the big dog like it was a Chihuahua. I walked closer. Only then did I see what the dog was guarding. I didn't know who it was at first, only that a man crouched at the side of the field. My body tensed involuntarily and I pulled the leashes to halt Chance and Sasha. I stood very still for a moment, debating whether to turn and walk quietly away from the bizarre scene or enter into it. I tied the girls to a dogwood tree and walked softly, moving closer to the figure.

I could not see his face until I was a few yards away, but I smelled the too sweet, pungent spice of aftershave. And I knew the man was Mr. Jake.

"Mr. Jake," I called. But he did not respond. He only stared straight ahead at the shepherd mix who had him cornered.

I walked closer to the dog and waved my arms casually. Flash let out a little *rep, rep* and I said, "Go on!" like I was speaking to a squirrel stealing birdseed, not a half-feral dog. I was surprised when the big dog looked at me but stood his ground. "*Go on!*" I shouted and made a lunge toward him. And that did it. The dog leapt to the side like I'd hit him with a cattle prod, then ran off into the surrounding woods.

I wasn't afraid of the neighbor's dogs. Those dogs were fearful if a stranger even so much as moved toward them. But I couldn't say I felt so calm about standing before Mr. Jake.

"They're all fraidy cats," I said conversationally to Mr. Jake, who was still crouching on the ground looking off at the spot where the dog had run. "Afraid of their own shadows unless they find out you're afraid." I was babbling then, no telling what I'd say next. *Flash hunts the mice in my house and once when I was*

192

sitting on the toilet a mouse ran right across—I started to speak again, but he turned his face toward me and I shut up.

I think for that instant the birds in the field and the leaves on the trees all stopped moving as Mr. Jake and I stared into each other's eyes. The feeling I'd had walking up to the field was growing stronger, and I realized it was a sense of knowing. I remember thinking that it should be impressed upon us in youth the importance of living in such a way that we can face our memories when old. Near-death survivors know this firsthand. The rest of us stumble and fall, vow to change bad habits, fail, then vow again. But like the sun breaking through a bank of clouds, sometimes one touch of love is enough to break down walls and transform even the most hardened heart.

And then I said it. From where it came, I didn't know. "It's not your fault, Mr. Jake." And at that moment his face changed so completely it looked like it belonged to someone else. I saw his eyes grow large like they'd been struck with the mallet of grief from many years ago, and his face contorted in anger, or maybe it was fear. Every human has something hidden, and it is perhaps these secrets that cause the most pain. Thinking no one else feels what we do, we dig trenches to bury our shame deeper still. In that instant I knew I no longer had to fear Mr. Jake. With Flash against my waist and the girls staring after us, I stepped toward the man, and held out my hand. Mr. Jake looked up at me, then he looked at Flash. I saw his eyes darken. I had seen that look before. Now I recognized it.

But I stood my ground, refusing to lower my hand until he reached out to take it. And finally he did. I pulled, trying to help him up. Then, with Mr. Jake towering over me, strained silence floated between us.

"My son was killed by a dog." He spoke the words to me but I heard no emotion in his voice. Perhaps it was all cried out. "I hate them all. And they know it. They sense it."

I squinted, trying to understand what was behind the words, but before I could attempt a reply Mr. Jake continued, "But your dog there was not the dog. You love your little dog the way I loved my son."

"I'm sorry," I said, looking into his dull blue eyes that still showed the fear I'd finally understood. "I'm so sorry."

He nodded. I saw him glance to the spot where the dog had run but the dog was gone. Then Mr. Jake turned and walked away, without telling us never to step foot on his land again. My heart was beating strong and alive. Then I was running back to Chance and Sasha and kissing them all over. How would I ever tell what had just happened to Nora?

That night I walked outside with Flash in my arms and looked up to the stars and there, shining above us, was Sirius, the dog star, the brightest star in the universe. "Shining for you," I said kissing the small black head. "Shining for you."

CHAPTER 36

Dual Realities

Any kind of expectation creates a problem. We should accept, but not expect. Whatever comes, accept it. Whatever goes, accept it. The immediate benefit is that your mind is always peaceful.

—SRI SWAMI SATCHIDANANDA

I REALIZE NOW WE DON'T ALWAYS GET WHAT WE WANT OR even what we think we need, but we get what is right. And I guess in the end it's not what we want, but rather what the universe wants for the highest good of all.

One afternoon Ted came over to give me company and perhaps some diversion. We sat outside as Chance and Sasha traced the edges of the fence, and Flash walked up and down the yard, sniffing the earth for rodents, his tail feathering behind him. It was a clear spring day. The sun touched the grass where we sat and I dug in the dirt with my left hand, letting the warm earth crumble through my fingers. A solitary jet was leaving a vertical contrail in the sky.

"I know it's because of the earth's atmosphere," I said, "but what an illusion. It always looks like one of those rides at the fair that go straight up and down, and the people ought to be scared hairless, their little plastic cups of soda water and peanuts all over their shoes."

We both stared at the plane's vertical ascent, wondering how much else in life seemed one thing but was in fact something else. Flash walked by us, his head swinging back and forth across the earth like one of those gadgets people use at the beach to seek out lost jewelry and coins. Or maybe he was like the Jains of India who brush the trail in front of them in order to save bugs and small beings from the tread of their step. He hunched a little as he walked, but apart from that and the shaved rectangle along his back (where, because the prednisone inhibited hair growth, the hair hadn't grown back) there was nothing to indicate he'd been sick.

"And it can teach tolerance," Ted said, eyes still on the jet.

"What?" I asked, then in the next instant I understood he meant the plane and nodded, for didn't we always believe our opinions the right ones, seeing often only one side while, no different from the ascending planes with merry reading-and-sleeping people within, multiple explanations and facets lay unspoken?

Martin Heidegger said there were really only four things we had to remember: Earth, Sky, Divinity, and Mortality. We are all of the earth and sky and all share it. Since we didn't make anything, remembering divinity helps us remember our size. Heidegger included mortality so that we would make the most of each day. The Native Americans had always known the importance of these things, and embroidered the motifs on blankets and teepees, but we of the modern world tended to forget.

When I was home in my small world with the dogs, the plants and the garden, the bugs and the mice, the trees and the yard, life made sense. Darkness giving way to dawn. Winter becoming spring. The birds and the bees and the natural world all fit together, and everything was perfect. There was always enough: enough food, enough water, enough peace, enough happiness. Each morning that I awoke and carried Flash from the bed and watched him shake his toy before breakfast or hunt up and down the yard searching for moles, there was a quiet sense of gratitude and joy. I was aware that Flash could not stay with us forever, yet somehow I knew this gift of peace he'd bestowed would remain.

Flash walked by again and I quoted to my literature-loving brother my favorite lines from the great poet Hafiz: "When all your desires are distilled / You will cast just two votes / To love more / And be happy."

Ted nodded. The plane was flying out of our view when he said, "There's a point at which science and spirit merge and the great masters and yogis have always known it. In their highest interpretations philosophy and mathematics merge. Maybe, in the end, great science and great art are the same. Both trying to answer the same questions: Why are we here? What is life's purpose? And how ultimately do we make sense of life and death?"

And then Flash was walking over to us and plunking down in his typical Flash-fashion. He stared up at me. I took off my watch and angled it so the sun hit the crystal. As I dragged the flash of light across the grass, he backed up and pounced. Then he was digging and taking big bites of earth.

I wanted this time to last forever. I wanted to watch Flash in his quest for the light and tell him something really profound about the way I felt. I wanted to express my feelings of love for my brother. I turned to him and saw him watching Flash dig, and saw the smile about his lips. I turned back to Flash.

"Get it, Flash," I said. "Get it."

CHAPTER 37

Accepting Miracles

All his reverence and all his fondness and all the leanings of his life were for the ardenthearted and they would always be so and never be otherwise.

—CORMAC MCCARTHY

IT WAS MARCH 29. I FED THE DOGS THEIR BREAKFAST, WHICH consisted of lightly sautéed organic, free-range meats, supplements, and Jason Winters tea for Flash. Afterward I sat on the floor to edit, leaning back against a chair. Sasha climbed onto me and pushed her nose against my hand to be petted. No sooner had she bumped my hand than a breeze came in from an open window and my papers fluttered up and around us. Two sheets of paper in particular sailed her way. She leapt off my lap like I'd told her she was next in line for a bath, and the look on her gentle face became confused with fear. I scooted to be next to her, reaching for her body and stroking her while her eyes still cast from side to side then up to the ceiling where once, long ago, bad things had come down from the sky.

"Sasha," I said softly. "Sweet Sasha, there's nothing to be afraid of." And as I said the words I realized how completely I believed them.

When I stood to gather my papers, I turned around and there was Flash outside in the yard on the wet grass of spring. Tears gathered in the back of my throat. I now found more tears filling my eyes from joy than had ever spilled over in pain. I found too that I measured time in smaller and smaller increments, the way people past one hundred speak of their age as "one hundred and one day, one hundred and three days." I've heard it said that animals don't fear death because they're not conscious of their mortality. I'm not sure this is true, but what I do think is that animals are less concerned about being in a physical body because they're connected to the universal consciousness in a way that we humans have lost or live unaware. If my own sense of mortality gave me anything, it was an urgency to live not only a life of some small meaning, but also a life of goodness. I felt life passing quickly. They are here for such a short time. . . .

I stood at the window watching Flash until the ringing phone broke my thoughts. I answered to the beautiful voice of Tanya, the Chechen cellist.

"Kay," she said, after we exchanged greetings. "You may have the painting you love." She was speaking of her husband's irreverent painting of the Madonna and the dachshund. "Sasha said he will reduce the price for you. You have always cared for Hassan and Mouza," she said, naming their two dachshunds, and somehow I felt Flash's slight touch in this. ". . . and you believe in art. We want the painting to go to someone who will love it."

She was practically giving it away to me. I argued, but she held firm. So I said I would buy another painting as well. We continued talking and catching up, but I was half listening; I was already picturing where I'd place the painting in my house.

I would hang the Madonna and dachshund in the living room so that it would be one of the first things people saw when they entered. I might lose a few friends, but I'd keep the ones who mattered.

"And how is Flash?" she asked, the name sounding both beautiful and funny the way she pronounced it.

"He's really good," I said to her smiling into the phone.

"He is a miracle," she said. "Protected by angels."

As the days passed and spring possessed the earth, Flash walked outside in air so gentle and soft, it seemed to sing a lullaby to him. Yes, it was a miracle, and yet a part of me had always known that this would come to be.

In *The Wisdom of the Sands*, St. Exupéry writes that "behind all seen things lies something vaster; everything is but a path, a portal, or a window opening onto something other than itself." Perhaps the time spent caring for Flash and learning how to become my best self was just that—a tiny window opening out to worlds of Eternity, for when I looked into each dog's eyes I saw something beyond the tangible world I knew of everyday jobs and routines. In their eyes I saw something for which I had no words.

Sometimes it is by remembering the anguish that we measure the joy. In the weeks that followed the first yellow flowers, there came days so golden in their purity that I knew the sense of peace would be enough to carry me through whatever long years might follow, no matter what they held. One such moment occurred as I typed at the computer while outside the white sheets billowed on the line, and through the reflection of the computer screen I could see the leaves of the silver maple doing the same. Lying by my feet, Flash stared up at me, love shining in his eyes, and in that moment, frozen in time like a snapshot, I knew a part of him would always be with me.

We pass through the horror, those moments we deem unutterable, only to emerge into sunlight and warmth. Each time we do, perhaps the hardship is lessened and we realize that this too, like all things, shall pass. For happiness doesn't lie in the depths of pleasure, but in something much quieter. *Heard melodies are sweet, but those unheard are sweeter.* Joy came to us many days through silence and stillness. I thanked the gods for the miracle of life. And I thanked Flash for the miracle of love.

CHAPTER 38

Return

The butterfly counts not the months, but the minutes, and has time enough for all.

—RABINDRANATH TAGORE

I HAVE NO IDEA WHAT INSPIRED ME TO SAY YES TO MARIE. IT must have been one of those I-feel-like-torture-today moods, for somehow she managed to talk me into going shopping with her at the mall in Short Pump, Virginia. Now if Dante were to get writer's block and ask me for help, I would ask him to consider in place of the blazing inferno in the seventh circle of hell, the shopping malls of North America. But I guess it's too late to rewrite history now.

I'm not a shopper. And then there was Flash. I didn't want one minute away from him. By this point I knew our days together were numbered. But Marie had been a loving presence to me, and as I was weighing my decision, I remembered that the veterinary clinic was ten minutes from Short Pump. It was then that the idea came to me: Flash was going shopping.

I raced to get his soft-sided traveling bag. I kissed Chance and Sasha on their heads and gave them biscuits. Then I was loading up Flash and thinking how we're all travelers on individual and uncompleted journeys and we never know how they'll turn out until they're over.

"Jesus, Mary, and Joseph," Marie said as we drove east toward Richmond. "I started a new diet and what do I get?"

"What," I said in the way you answer a knock-knock joke.

"I gained four pounds."

"Oh Marie!" I began, wanting somehow to help her, but before I could begin she continued.

"I know what I have to do."

This time I waited.

"It's not about what I eat. I need to love myself. I've heard it a million times, but I think this time, it's finally sinking in. We all need to love ourselves."

I nodded. Of course we all did. But sometimes it was easier to jog up Mount Everest.

"I spend time with my family, and they drive me crazy but I love them so much. I want to be able to talk to them, but I don't seem to ever get through."

I reached over and squeezed her arm.

"Say something. Anything," she beseeched me.

"All higher communication begins in the heart." I'd read it somewhere, but now I knew it firsthand. "In order to find peace, look to your heart." I offered her back her own advice.

"I can't find my heart for all the fat around it."

"Marie!"

"I keep blaming everyone but myself."

I glanced in the rearview mirror to Flash and listened.

"It's not my family's fault. I just can't seem to accept that I've created the mess I'm in."

"Yeah, and it's too bad you're the only person in the world who has this problem."

"Shut up. Like you're any better, loving a . . . *wiener dog* the way you do!"

"I love you too."

"Love you more."

"The Beatles had it right, I think. Love is all you need."

"You think?"

"I do."

"Do me a favor," Marie interrupted. "Reach over like you did just then and hold my arm. I don't have anyone to touch me or hug me."

I reached over again and gently squeezed her arm, and she grasped on to me hard and didn't let go for a good while.

When we arrived at the mall, I let Marie out in front of Trader Joe's and we arranged a meeting time. I drove back to the veterinary referral center, to the place I had first been told the news of Flash's cancer. I pulled up to the brick building and turned off the ignition. Flash looked up at me from inside his bag. His eyes were bright. He still had the shaved strip along his back where the hair was extra soft to the touch, a reminder of his day here five months ago. But, this time his neck was not stiff and, when I looked at him, there was no angst written between his eyes.

I walked around to the passenger side and slung his bag over my shoulder. As I was walking in I saw the white pine standing out by the grass. I remembered how it had reminded me of Lauren and given hope on that day, which now seemed a long time ago. I remembered the fall leaves scattered around it but now saw only new green grass.

Strange as it felt to be walking up to the Veterinary Referral Center where I had spent so much difficult time, the moment held joy and what I can only describe, in that uncertain land of time and memory, as a moment of contented maturity—moments of peace, born of knowing you could survive the worst.

I had not made an appointment but I asked to see my doctor anyway. I wanted to show her Flash. The receptionist said she would ask and told me to sit down. As I sat and held Flash on my lap, I remembered that day in November when time seemed interminable and death cast its shadow across our lives. I looked around the familiar room. There were two other people waiting, a man and a woman, but neither had an animal with them. I guess they were waiting for news.

I sat a long time stroking Flash as he peeked out from the bag. I wondered if he remembered it all as I remembered it. Finally a receptionist told me the doctor could not come, but that I could talk with a technician. I stood up to follow her back, but she motioned for me to sit, explaining that the tech would come to me.

I felt the embarrassment of telling my story before others, and was about to leave when the tech walked out. I recognized her as someone who had helped us before. I spoke quickly, not wanting to prolong her day. I explained Flash's diagnosis of two to three weeks at the very most. She stared at me and I could see the amazement take shape across her face.

"I remember him," she said reaching out a hand to touch his back. "It really doesn't seem possible. What'd you do?"

I spoke to her about the physical remedies that I thought she would appreciate with her medical background. Then I said, "I guess it was a miracle. A miracle born of love."

She said nothing for a moment, then smiled. "I believe that. That's when I know an animal is going to heal. Well, I gotta go.

Thanks for sharing that. We see a lot of tragedy. It's nice to see some triumph. I'll tell Dr. Luster."

I was almost to the car when I felt the slightest touch on my shoulder. I turned and there was a woman behind me. Preoccupied with comparing past to present, I'd neither seen nor heard her approach.

"Excuse me," she began, and as she did another memory surfaced—the woman with the little white dog. For a split second, I imagined she was telling me her dog had survived. Then I realized she'd been talking and I hadn't heard.

"I'm sorry, you reminded me of someone else," I apologized.

"I heard you say in there that it was a miracle, and . . . I need a miracle . . . I need . . ."

I heard the desperation in her voice. I was looking back at her but all I could say was, "A miracle?"

"Yes." Now she was hesitant, embarrassed. But she persisted. "Is there anything special . . . I mean how do you receive miracles? Is there something concrete that I could do?"

I said nothing for a moment, gauging the proper response. What did she need? I saw her hungry, fearful face. She needed the same things we all needed. Then I began, "This is going to sound weird but . . ."

"Nothing will sound weird. Please."

"Well, I think it starts with your heart. You try to open your heart."

"Open my heart?"

"Yes. Live from your heart. Love all you can. Love everyone and everything you can."

"That doesn't sound weird at all," she answered.

I told her as briefly and as undramatically as I could about Flash. Even the biggest skeptics couldn't argue with the fact that Flash was hopping through the spring flowers when his death sentence in early November had been the more likely probability.

I felt compelled to share with her everything I'd done and everything I knew. I told her the fastest method I knew of opening your heart was to feel gratitude for every little thing—not only the momentous events, but simple occasions: smelling the aroma of baking baguettes in the predawn hours of Paris, or listening to someone all alone in the apartment next door playing the piano really well. Looking into your dog's soft brown eyes. Smelling the scent of one single rose.

I was on a roll and started talking about one of my favorite scenes in drama, a scene from—perhaps not so coincidentally—her favorite play, *Our Town*. The scene is the last one, when Emily gets the chance to return from the grave to view her life on earth one last time, and she says:

> Good-bye, good-bye, world. Good-bye, Grover's Corners . . .
> Mama and Papa. Good-bye to clocks ticking . . . and Mama's
> sunflowers. And food and coffee. And new-ironed dresses and
> hot baths . . . and sleeping and waking up! Oh, earth, you're too
> wonderful for anybody to realize you! Do any human beings
> ever realize life while they live it? Every, every minute?

"I love that scene!" the woman said. "I never would have thought of evoking that to bring me my miracle," she smiled.

I told her it was essential that we quiet our minds. The sun was warm on my face, and as I stroked Flash's back I realized how happy I felt just standing there. I glanced across the spring grass to the pine again. "Maybe the most important thing to receiving the miracles life has for us is to realize that now is the only time there is and that each moment is beautiful. And maybe a miracle is nothing more than being able to see life standing before you."

"I feel it," she answered and reached a tentative hand out to Flash. "May I?" she asked. "May I touch your little miracle?"

"Sure," I laughed. "He loves it."

Flash preened as the woman stroked his head, and as I stood in the parking lot with Flash and the woman who needed a miracle I realized perhaps I had come full circle. I was not mouthing platitudes that one could find in any self-help book; I had internalized them and I was living them. Flash moved about in the bag then stuck his two front feet out. I set him on the ground and watched him scamper off after a bird.

"Thank you," the woman said to me. "You and your miracle dog there have just changed my life. I feel it. I know it." And as she said it, I almost felt I knew it too. I saw the tears in her eyes and I reached out to hug her.

"You have a dog in there?"

"A cat," she answered, and I saw different tears wet her eyes then.

"What is his or her name?"

"His name is Cherub."

"Cherub?"

"Yes." She smiled at me guiltily.

"What's he look like?"

"He's black and white. He's beautiful."

"I'm sure he is." I smiled into her eyes, wishing I could ease her worry. "I'll think of Cherub. I'll send him love."

"Thank you."

We said good-bye, and I realized I'd most likely never see this woman again. But we had touched each other's hearts, and that was enough. I turned and saw Flash sitting by the little pine tree.

Chapter 39

Easter

Leaves that the wind drives earthward, such are the generations of men.

—Homer

That year Easter Sunday was on April 4.

I was standing out in the yard in the afternoon thinking how Flash was still alive when a bluebird flew past us. I saw Flash watch him with what looked like envy, but perhaps that was only my anthropomorphic interpretation. Maybe Flash only saw bluebird stew.

Sometimes we don't understand a message until days or even years later. In *Animal Speak,* Ted Andrews writes that the bluebird is a symbol of happiness. Although feisty if their mates or nestlings are threatened, bluebirds are otherwise gentle and nonaggressive. As a result their nests are often taken over by more assertive birds. In Virginia we have special trails with bluebird houses and baffles on the houses to keep out snakes and encourage the dwindling bluebird population. While once common throughout North America, bluebirds are now somewhat rare. Andrews suggests this is a reminder that "we are born to happiness and fulfillment, but we sometimes get so lost and wrapped up in the everyday events of our lives that happiness and fulfillment seem rare."

As the late-afternoon light touched the flowering trees, I dipped each of the dogs' front feet in water-soluble paint and stamped green paw prints up the white steps to my Writing Room. I wrote each name next to the set of paw prints, with Flash's on the top step with the date. Then I rinsed their feet clean.

Perhaps the years would see these marks washing off with each new rain, but for a while at least the prints would bring me comfort. Edna St. Vincent Millay wrote, "But I shall find the sullen rocks and skies / Unchanged from what they were when I was young."

There is a constancy in some forms of nature that can trick us into believing things don't change. I now know that what remains unchanged throughout the years is the love and respect we give back to others. For if life mirrors our innermost thoughts, all the fears and all the love, I think what survives in the end is the love. And perhaps there really is a benevolent god whose kind tricks of memory allow us to remember only the good. If the love of a dog can tap into the mystical realm of not only my heart but the world's infinite wisdom, then I'm all for it and what does it matter what anyone says?

There are certain moments in life that live in our memories throughout our lives. A wedding day, a fabled trip, or simply a Sunday afternoon cookout spent with family. That one lazy Easter afternoon in April was one such memory forever woven into the tapestry of my life.

Another occurred that same evening as I lay on the sofa with Flash draped across my stomach like linguine. Chance and Sasha lay squashed up against my legs. Bach's Mass in B minor played, and I knew that when I traveled through the long years ahead, I could always remember that on one night, Easter, I was holding him in my arms.

CHAPTER **40**

April

There are four questions of value in life: What is sacred? Of what is the spirit made? What is worth living for? And what is worth dying for? The answer to each one is the same. Only love.

—JEREMY LEVEN

THAT APRIL FOUND US OFTEN IN THE WRITING ROOM. ONE day Flash slept beside Chance and Sasha on the couch. The breeze floated in and gently raised the papers on my desk but Sasha did not jump in panic. The jingle of the wind chimes combined with the sounds of birds calling back and forth, and created a natural symphony from which emanated the sound of life itself. Mating season.

I slipped from behind my desk and sat down beside the dogs. I thought back to the cold and hardened days of winter. After those long months of patchy, piled snow, how was it possible that grass shimmered green beneath my bare feet? How was it possible that flowers broke through the once frozen earth? Flash opened his eyes and flipped over on his back. From his upside-down position he peered up at me, the whites of his eyes showing and his overbite most obvious. I rubbed his smooth tummy. And how was this possible?

The quince at the foot of Flash's ramp was a festival of dark, bawdy pink, and I hoped that St. Francis, standing beside it, felt its joy and its warmth. The almond tree had begun the same ritual, opening, offering and unfolding each pink petal. The plums turned toward the new season, seductive sirens to the bees who buzzed and hovered and feasted deep on nectar. Beside them stood Flash's cherry tree, the one that had never bloomed in all the years we'd lived there. Until that year. Its soft blossoms like the touch and feel of kindness.

And then there was the viburnum. The viburnum underneath whose dark fall leaves I had cried—wondering how I'd bear the spring.

I needed only to look around to see the miracle of life, returning to us each year. At dusk there was the chorus of peepers beyond our windows. There were the bats which fluttered and swooped, and the swallows making arcs in the dim light. There was the soft smell of earth and evening air, and of the cool cut grass I knew as a child. And for those short, fleeting days there was the scent of the viburnum. Its exotic sweetness came to me once a year, its soft, scented flowers now symbolic to me of Flash and the full cycle he had made from November to spring.

CHAPTER 41

Death

There is a land of the living and a land of the dead and the bridge is love, the only survival, the only meaning.
—THORNTON WILDER

T. S. ELIOT WROTE THAT "APRIL IS THE CRUELEST MONTH, breeding lilacs out of the dead land, mixing memory and desire, stirring dull roots with spring rain," and while Eliot wrote of war, I write of Flash, yet still concur that maybe life consists of not always getting exactly what we want, but in recognizing the value of what we've been given.

April 14 was a soft day, the kind of day that uplifts human thought and spirit. Light, cottony clouds drifted across a blue sky that seemed to promise more of everything beautiful and good. Chance and Sasha stood midway down the yard and Flash was sniffing in the grass beside the garden which wrapped itself around the house, offering a bounty of veggies to us more than half the year long. Ted was with me in the living room, and as we looked out the large windows we could observe all three dogs living lives independent from us.

I had just taken a sip of tea when I glanced out to where Flash was standing. Ted must have followed my habitual gaze, for when I turned, we both remarked in almost identical phrasing, "Flash is acting strange. Flash is not himself."

Flash snapped at the air, then turned and ran at something neither Ted nor I could see. Together we stood watching, hesitating about what to do. Flash's hind end collapsed and he remained sitting in the grass, still trying to chase his tormentors. I ran outside and called to him. He pushed up and scampered toward me, but his hindquarters had no coordination. As though confused, he ran back and snapped at the air, jerking this way and that. He didn't seem in pain, but I could not understand his odd behavior.

"Flash!" I called again, and he came my way. But again he stopped and hopped back to take care of, once and for all, whatever or whomever was bothering him.

Back in the house he would have looked like a normal, happy dog to anyone else but me. With pricked ears, he was exceptionally alert, but he was just the slightest bit . . . off.

Ted left and I set Flash up on the armchair beside Chance and I took his picture. He looked handsome, but wrinkled creases questioned between his eyes and spoke of confusion and, with his lined agitation, I sensed he was not the Flash I had known for thirteen years.

I carried him to the bed. Chance and Sasha joined us and together we lay down for a nap. It was a pause, a caesura, a beat in time whose significance came to me only afterward. Flash rested his head across my arm. Sasha lay against my thigh and Chance slept next to her. The breeze came through the open window, and as I drifted in and out of gentle sleep I could not have foretold that this would be one of our last beautiful moments together.

What happened next was like a bad dream, something that happens only in other people's lives. I made a sandwich and ate my lunch quietly at the dining room table. When I finished I set the plate on the floor for the dogs to lick clean together as they had done so many times.

When I turned back around, I saw Flash. He was bent at a right angle and jerking in spasms. Even though I'd never before witnessed this scene, I knew he was dying. I took two steps toward him, dropped to the ground, and placed my hands on either side of him, holding him, speaking slowly and softly.

"I'm here, Flash. I'm here," I said. "I love you. I'm right here with you. I love you. *Oh God.*" I remained calm for his sake, but tears began filling my eyes. I spoke only three words to him. But I spoke them over and over and over. "I love you."

The seizure subsided after four or five minutes and Flash lay dazed. In the dog bed by the window he shut his eyes, and as I sat down beside him, the sunlight came in through the window and covered him. During this quiet spell I made phone calls trying to figure out what to do. Then he was up and walking through a quiet space of hope, a slight drool coming from his mouth. When I centered myself, I heard the words *air and light*. I packed Flash up into the knapsack, clipped leashes on the girls, and headed for the river. Together we walked through the soft, cool air as the leaves above us spoke of the secrets that only they knew.

The light danced and sparkled on the water's rippled surface. I marveled how one moment the water could be turbulent, the next moment calm. As I stood listening to the song of the river, I could feel Flash's warm body against my own. I dipped my hands into the river's cold breath as I always did and touched his long thin muzzle, a baptism of all that had been and all that was yet to be. I ran my hands over his shaved back, and it was one of those moments in which what's eternal shines through time and, for that instant, we see through the illusion.

Then we turned around. On the way home I looked to the spot where, a few weeks after his surgery, I had set him on the ground and seen him walk the couple paces on his own. I'd been filled with elation then. Now, as I walked softly, I felt a quiet sense of contentment that we were all walking through sunlight and shadow together, a gentle peace and gratitude for the time I'd been granted with him. I didn't know that this would be our last walk together.

The seizure never completely broke and Flash endured another and another with intermittent twitching in between. I took him to the emergency vets that evening. By then, after heavy doses and injections of Valium and phenobarbital, Flash was unresponsive. The vet at the emergency clinic explained that he would not recover; the seizure had gone on too long. He suggested we put him to sleep right away instead of taking the chance that he would die by seizing. Or, if not, he advised that Flash should stay the night, monitored under supervision.

"I'm not putting him down here," I said, holding him in my arms.

I said I would not euthanize him in an unfamiliar veterinary hospital and that he would come back to the love and comfort of his own home, at least for one last night. I said I'd monitor him myself, a risky proposition at best as he could endure another seizure during the night, from which he could die a difficult death. At no time more than now did I need to have the faith I'd sought so hard to understand.

By then I knew that this was Flash's last night. By then I knew that I would have to euthanize him in the morning if he did not die in the night. And just how do you do that? How do you make the one decision that is harder than all the rest to make? How do you end the physical life of a being you love more than you have words to express, taking another's life into your own hands? How can you? Because you love him, that is how.

I called Dr. Strozum, and by another miracle he was home and willing to come to my house the next morning so that Flash could depart from the physical world in the peace of his own bed.

That night the three dogs and I lay huddled in vulnerable disbelief and I stroked Flash throughout the night. His sides heaved up and down and I spoke to him of all the places we had been together: There was Paris, Nice, Villefranche . . . the Eden Roc on the Cap d'Antibes, the beach many times, camping, sneaking into restaurants and hotels, being kicked out of restaurants and hotels.

Then there were the small moments in between that would make his leaving us so hard to bear. Flash at home doing what he loved most: rooting around the yard, chasing butterflies, hunting for moles. I thought of his black body there amongst the Christmas wrapping paper, then standing beside the first flowers of spring. Flash in bed beside Chance and Sasha, beside me. Flash at Susie's. Flash snapping up cookies with his huge overbite. Flash begging for food while on steroids. And Flash singing.

I thought of how he would lie in the dog bed before the woodstove in his older years, but not before first flipping up the blanket with his head and crawling underneath; how he would seek out the spots of sunshine in the house and follow the light from place to place; how he would scratch the earth with his front feet digging for moles and take giant bites of dirt; how he would try to dig up my hardened floor tiles seeking the elusive mice; how he, always a beacon of lighthearted fun, would try to mount Chance or Sasha and instigate play; and how he would chase the reflection of my watch or any other flash of light for hours, enjoying the moment with never a need to eat his quarry or reach some arbitrary goal.

My eyes bathed him in love as I looked at his long nose with its short black whiskers, the folded ears, the funny feet I loved. There was his body and long tail, and his left front leg now wrapped in blue tape. I tried to study and to memorize what in a few short hours would be taken from me and I would never see again. I sang to him his funny song, "He's so fine, he's so fine. And I'm so glad that he's all mine." And as the tears wet my face I tried to listen with my heart.

That last night together held the greatest miracle of all—which is simply this: to be with another in the darkest hour, without the need to speak. To simply sit and offer love. And if loving costs us pain and sorrow, not loving always costs us more. One of life's greatest gifts is to have known such a tender and uncomplicated love, even if that same love is taken away all too soon.

"You'll be with us always," I told him, trying to believe my own words. Perhaps by then he felt and knew the truth better than I did. He seemed at once far away and yet very close to me.

He slept the night next to me in his subdued narcotic slumber and never broke into another seizure. Marveling at this miracle, I stroked his tired body. Sometimes I made small Tellington TTouch circles with my fingers. I sang his song and covered him with kisses, whispering again and again the words he must have known by then so well, "I love you, Flash. I love you."

They were easy words to speak, originating from my heart and falling from my lips along with my tears. The few words I had learned less well were easy too. Still they choked me up. "Good-bye, Flash. It's okay to go."

When the first light of morning came I was scared. I had wanted the night to last. I placed my arms beneath his fragile body and gently lifted him. I carried him outside to feel the sun and air one last time. Brown saliva covered the pillow and I noticed the tiniest indentation where his head had lain. With him resting in my arms, I squatted amongst the flowers we had planted in the fall. There was sacredness in our smallest acts. Everything we did together now was for the last time, a strange sensation. The sun touched us both and I thought of two lives oddly entwined and now forever connected by love. Together we stepped up on the old apple crate. The fields and woods lay hushed in morning light and I felt them honoring a small dog who had loved to look out to the lands beyond. At last I picked a big white viburnum blossom and carried Flash back inside. I lay him on the bed, his head upon my pillow. Sunlight touched his back and a gentle breeze came in. Then the light was all around him, and I felt a strange peace. Chance and Sasha jumped up on the bed and I lay the white viburnum across his black and shiny shoulder.

When I heard the car wheels outside on the gravel, I breathed in and out slowly but I was trembling. Chance and Sasha barked and Flash raised his head and looked around.

"*I love you, Flash,*" I whispered to him. "*I love you so much.*"

Then Dr. Strozum and his wife, Shay, were walking in, bringing with them a kind and quiet energy. The girls lay pressed together at the foot of the bed like quiet sentinels, though very much aware of what was going on, and I sat next to Flash. I kissed his face and eyes.

"Don't be afraid, Flash. I love you, Flash."

Then Sid injected him as I stroked his tired body. His sides rose up and down and with each breath the viburnum rose as if moved by the breeze. His breathing was slightly labored but he seemed at peace. Then he was not breathing anymore. I watched as his body became an empty vessel, no longer filled with life, and I knew the moment he had gone. Outside, the birds called back and forth and the spring flowers stood blooming. But the viburnum across his back lay still. That is how he left the world we four had known together. Courageously and with great dachshund dignity.

EPILOGUE

The Silver Lining

And now here is my secret, a very simple secret: It is only with the heart that one can see rightly. What is essential is invisible to the eye.

—ANTOINE DE ST. EXUPÉRY

THE DAY AFTER FLASH DIED I AWOKE AND LOOKED FOR THE indentation his head had left on the pillow, but it was gone. The sun rose over the mountain and I went about my daily tasks. The routine of simple chores grounded me, while at the same time intensifying the grief. People were rising and driving to work: another ordinary day. But a light had turned off in my world.

Unable to write in the Writing Room, I sat at the desk in my office and answered mundane e-mails. A beautiful woman I'd known for a long time, if incidentally, sent an e-mail telling me she'd recently separated from her husband of many years. I was moved by her capacity to share her vulnerability with me, and wrote back explaining to her about Flash. Yet the words felt empty. Somehow the act of writing, "Flash died by my side yesterday morning," or "I just lost my little dachshund of thirteen years yesterday," could not begin to convey what I felt. But the act of sharing, particularly to this kindhearted woman, soothed me.

222

In the afternoon I called to Chance and Sasha, and together we crouched in the grass staring at the earth and her flowers. A memory came to me then unbidden: A shiny black dachshund, digging up dirt as I laughed in my attempt to plant fall bulbs on his birthday.

When grief is strong, it feels as if joy will never return. But I sat still and did not try to push away my sorrow. Kahlil Gibran writes:

Your joy is your sorrow unmasked.
And the selfsame well from which your laughter
rises was oftentimes filled with your tears.
And how else can it be?
The deeper that sorrow carves into your being,
the more joy you can contain.

I knew there would come a day when I would stand amongst the flowers of spring and feel joy that I had shared my life with such a special soul. But for the moment I felt empty and lost.

I waited for a sign that his spirit was nearby. I'd had discussions into the nature of the soul with many people over the years. I remember asking a wise friend about the soul's life after our bodies cease. And she said to me, "All those who are loved live on." I liked that idea and like to think that all beings feel love once in their lives. If not, I send them my love now. "I love you, Flash. Live on."

That night, a thousand stars were visible in the night sky in shades of blue, orange, yellow, pink, and white, but Sirius, the dog star, was gone.

The days were soft and beautiful. I bumbled through my work and chores, trying to keep appointments I'd made, trying to conceal my sadness at times, trying to remember things I said I'd do. What I remembered all too well was how he would wobble when he walked; how he ate, standing with roached back and cow hocks; how he sang the most beautiful songs; and how he looked at me with love in his eyes. I looked to my photos, but they were not him. There was his bowl. There was the dog bed by the woodstove where he once had lain.

What I wanted was simple: to look into his eyes and stroke him one more time. But I would never stroke him again. I wanted to hear him sing one more song. But Flash had sung his last song.

"Flash?" I called into the still, dense air. "Flash, where are you?" I felt something brush against my calf and glanced down. Staring up at me were two dark chocolate eyes and a cream face. Chance. I knelt down beside her and looked deep into her eyes.

Only then did I see what my own grief had prevented me from seeing until now. There in her eyes, for one fleeting moment, I saw all the love and all the pain. I saw what I had thought impossible: a grief deeper even than my own.

"*Oh, Chance.*" I knelt to be next to her. "*Chance,*" I whispered again to the one who'd known him perhaps better than all. Sasha trotted up to join us and I let my hands run over their warm and living bodies, while my tears wet the fur on the tops of their heads.

"I'm so sorry. You loved him too. I know, I know. Oh, how is he not here with us?" With the wisdom unique to them, my two girls answered me: Flash was with us still. He was there in the first notes of the song. He was there in the touch of the breeze. He was there in the sparkling light on the river's back.

I remembered how I would call to him when upset: "*Flash, right now!*" Squatting there, I let go of my own pain and I closed my eyes, breathing in the moment where I was. And it was then that I heard the words through my heart. *I am with you . . . right now.*

As spring turned into summer I tried to imagine what it would have been like to have him there with me. Then I remembered that I had been unable to imagine him beyond spring. Together he and I had received all that my human mind could dare believe.

Because so much of my day had gone into caring for him, there now seems huge gaps in time. On one particular day, I sat down outside as Chance and Sasha walked over to be near me.

"I love you, Chance. I love you, Sasha." I looked up to the sky and out to the fields where he and I would gaze together.

"*Flash,*" I whispered. "Where are you, Flash?" As I sat very still, breathing in the soft morning air, I heard at first faintly, then louder the notes of the wind chimes—even though there was not one ounce of breeze. A kind of peace settled over me then, cohabitating with my sorrow. At my feet I saw the heart-shaped leaves of the violets. Climbing up the fence I saw the morning glories, purple, blue, and pink. Interlaced among the flowers were large and small heart-shaped leaves. Perfect symmetrical hearts. And then there was the giant sunflower, towering over all of us and turning its smiling face toward the sun, loving its height and surveying the fields beyond.

I began to notice hearts everywhere. There were the morning glories, the moonflowers, the violets, the red buds and paulownias; I saw heart-shaped leaves on the zucchini and the grapevine; I found hearts in the rocks beneath my feet as we walked, following familiar trails over which I once had carried him.

It was during these times, when I was filled with love, that I first began to feel Flash. Perhaps he was with us, hunting and singing, merely existing at a higher frequency we couldn't see . . . but we could feel. And I realized on what a tiny linear scope we humans functioned when so much of life lay just beyond the veil.

And so, with the passage of time and by accepting life as it lived through me, I came to understand that Flash was still right there. Just as with Lauren, in my grief I had blocked myself from feeling him. I knew that grief and fear operated on much lower frequencies than love. When, with time, the sorrow of missing his physical presence eased, I was able to feel great joy, and with that came the ability to sense his spirit. I was living on the frequency of love.

One night I stood beneath the twinkling stars, looking up, searching for the answers that eluded me by day. For a long time I just stared up to the shimmering lights so far away and beautiful to behold. As the starlight soaked through me I remembered that the stars I see at night are still there by day; I just cannot see them.

In the end, I realize that the true miracle was more than Flash's prolonged health and life. The miracle was the wisdom I gained within myself, a deeper knowledge that we are all part of the same universe, eternal and evolving, connected at our best by love. We all experience pain, but sometimes it's that very pain which serves as the sand that forms the pearls within us. The more I felt love, the more I was able to feel Flash right there . . . rooting around in my heart.

One soft day as Chance and Sasha chewed on bones out in the yard, I walked down the steps from the Writing Room beside Flash's long ramp. I paused to look at his small paw prints at the top of the steps from that Easter Sunday afternoon. As my mind remembered him, I let my heart remember too and I felt a lump form in my throat. Just then a bluebird buzzed the top of my head and perched a foot from me in a young honey locust tree. It chirped as if speaking to me and I stood and smiled. Then it buzzed by my head a second time and returned to the same branch to look back at me.

I felt a strange tingling along my spine and down my arms. A memory. Someone speaking. I stood there and stared at the bluebird who was staring back at me, letting the words come: *He wants to be reincarnated and come back in a healthy body, maybe a bird, a happy, bluebird and fly high in the sky.* It was Rebecca's voice. *If he must make a choice . . . if he cannot stay and be comfortable. He loves you and would want to stay close by.*

The hair on the back of my neck prickled and I felt my eyes tear. I saw that there would always be a vast universe whose mechanisms my mind might never fully grasp but whose miracles my heart had long ago befriended.

I walked out to the grass and sat down by Chance and Sasha. When I begin to doubt and lose faith I close my eyes and ask my heart for an answer. It doesn't take long to feel love for a little black dachshund. And if I feel love for these dogs, mustn't I extend love to all dogs, all life?

I remembered another afternoon in the grass with the dogs just after I had given Flash the steroids and he'd sung with the siren. How he had revived and dug in the dirt. The memory now brought me comfort. The Buddhists have a saying: "What did you do before you became enlightened?"

The answer: "Split wood and carried water."

"And after becoming enlightened?"

"Split wood and carried water."

I'd been splitting wood and carrying water quite literally, for the woodstove and the plants, for a long time and I was happy to continue. It fed my soul in a way the Buddhists understand.

As I sat in the grass I heard the birds singing in the trees. Sasha climbed up onto me like I was a jungle gym. Chance leaned into me. I felt the warm earth beneath me. I felt the fur on Chance and Sasha as I stroked them. These were small things but they were enough. I was alive on a beautiful, ordinary day. I stood up ready to go on, the memory of a little black dog forever with me.

I remembered the email the day after Flash died, from the woman with the kind heart. She was as beautiful as she was loving, and in my grief I had responded back to her then forgotten about it. It was only after she emailed again, inviting me over, that I began to see the interconnectedness of all things. Only then did I realize that perhaps Flash had had a hand . . . or paw . . . in this. And as I put my fingers to the keyboard to respond, I glanced to the loveseat where long ago he had sat nudging my hand, distorting my writing and entering my heart.

I know now that it is only with our hearts that we can see clearly. Sometimes life breaks them open, but that's okay. When a heart breaks open, it lets in love. And it is only with our hearts wide open that we can begin to know the miracle of love.

In the late afternoon, I stood by the kitchen sink and watched the birds pecking at seeds. Time stopped. I saw Flash surrounded by spring flowers. The sky stretched out blue into infinity and my heart felt filled with joy. I called to Chance and Sasha and clipped on their leashes. And as we walked down the road through the patchy sunlight I had this beautiful, peaceful sense that everything works out exactly as it's meant. Behind us, the wind chimes began to sing softly.

"Thank you, Flash. Thank you for that beautiful song."

I am with you still
I do not sleep.
I am the thousand winds that blow,
I am the diamond glints in snow.
I am the sunlight on ripened grain,
I am the gentle autumn rain.
When you awaken in morning's hush
I am the swift uplifting rush
Of quiet birds in circled flight.
I am the soft stars that shine at night.
Do not think of me as gone.
I am with you still in each new dawn.
—Mary Elizabeth Frye

AFTERWORD

Some readers like to know about the author, while I think more readers like to know, "What happened next?" Well, Olive happened next.

Olive is an all-black, long-haired dachshund who came into our lives two years after Flash left us. She was so weak and exhausted she could not stand. Her condition involves a lack of pancreatic digestive enzymes, which doesn't allow her to absorb food. With enzymes, Olive is a happy, normal dog. Without them she will die. Signs of this condition are large,

mashed potato–like stools. Olive continues the tradition of rescued dachshunds as Chance and Sasha continue the tradition of rescued beagles. Olive is not Flash and will never replace Flash. She is her own dog, just as Chance is and Sasha is and Flash was and Lauren was. Each soul is worthy of love. However, not all animals receive the kind of love our animal companions receive. Profits from *Flash's Song* are donated to helping such animals, and I am committed to helping not only the dogs and cats who are neglected, abandoned, or abused, but also domestic animals used in factory farming and laboratory testing. For more information and a list of charities I support, see www.kaypfaltz.com.

———————

Below please find contact information about animal communication, total body analysis, and photography as mentioned in the book:

Susie Hoffman—total body analysis, sdhoffman@ntelos.net.

Rebecca Moravec—animal communication, www.kindredspiritsanimalcommunication.com. Contact Carolee Biddle, animalconnections@gmail.com, or visit http://www.animal-connections.com.

Amelia Kinkade—animal communication workshops, www.ameliakinkade.com.

Ted Pfaltz—professional pet portraits (and general photography), www.Maxxis7.com, Tedpfaltz@yahoo.com.